♉   THE TAURUS ENIGMA   ♉

Cracking the Code

The Zodiac Code series

THE
TAURUS
ENIGMA

Cracking the Code

JANE RIDDER-PATRICK

MAINSTREAM
PUBLISHING
EDINBURGH AND LONDON

For my brother Alan

First published in Great Britain in 2004 by
MAINSTREAM PUBLISHING COMPANY
(EDINBURGH) LTD
7 Albany Street
Edinburgh EH1 3UG

ISBN 1 84018 526 0

A catalogue record for this book is available
from the British Library

Typeset in Allise and Van Dijck

Printed in Great Britain by
Cox & Wyman Ltd

Contents

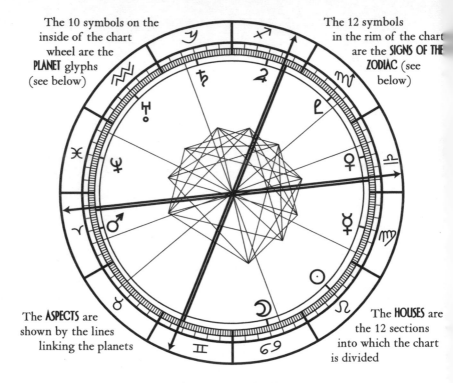

The 10 symbols on the inside of the chart wheel are the **PLANET** glyphs (see below)

The 12 symbols in the rim of the chart are the **SIGNS OF THE ZODIAC** (see below)

The **ASPECTS** are shown by the lines linking the planets

The **HOUSES** are the 12 sections into which the chart is divided

A Sample Birth Chart

Sign	Ruler	Sign	Ruler
Aries ♈	Mars ♂	Libra ♎	Venus ♀
Taurus ♉	Venus ♀	Scorpio ♏	Pluto ♇
Gemini ♊	Mercury ☿	Sagittarius ♐	Jupiter ♃
Cancer ♋	Moon ☽	Capricorn ♑	Saturn ♄
Leo ♌	Sun ☉	Aquarius ♒	Uranus ♅
Virgo ♍	Mercury ☿	Pisces ♓	Neptune ♆

ONE

The Truth of Astrology

MOST PEOPLE'S FIRST EXPERIENCE OF ASTROLOGY IS THROUGH newspapers and magazines. This is a mixed blessing for astrology's reputation – writing an astrology column to any degree of accuracy is a tough, many would say impossible, challenge. The astrologer has to try to say something meaningful about conditions that affect every single person belonging to the same sign, over a very short period of time, in a scant handful of words. The miracle is that some talented astrologers do manage to get across a tantalising whiff of the real thing and keep readers coming back for more of what most of us are hungry for – self-knowledge and reassurance about the future. The downside of the popularity of these columns is that many people think that all astrology is a branch of the entertainment industry and is limited to light-hearted fortune-telling. This is far from the truth.

What Astrology Can Offer
Serious astrology is one of the most sophisticated tools available to help us understand ourselves and the world

around us. It gives us a language and a framework to examine and describe – quite literally – *anything* under the Sun, from countries to companies, from money markets to medical matters. Its most common application, however, is in helping people to understand themselves better using their own unique birth charts. Astrology has two main functions. One is to describe the traits and tendencies of whatever it is that is being examined, whether this is a state, a software company or someone's psyche. The other is to give an astonishingly accurate timetable for important changes within that entity. In the chapters that follow, we'll be using astrology to investigate the psychology of the innermost part of your personality, taking a look at what drives, inspires and motivates you.

Astrology uses an ancient system of symbols to describe profound truths about the nature of life on earth, truths that cannot be weighed and measured, but ones we recognise nevertheless, and that touch and move us at a deep level. By linking mythology and mathematics, astrology bridges the gap between our inner lives and our outer experiences, between mind and matter, between poetry and science.

Fate and Free Will

Some people think that astrology is all about foretelling the future, the implication being that everything is predestined and that we have no say in how our lives take shape. None of that is true. We are far from being helpless victims of fate. Everything that happens to us at any given time is the result of past choices. These choices may have been our own, or made by other people. They could even have been made long ago before we, or even our grandparents, were born. It is not always possible to prevent processes that were set in motion in the past from coming to their logical conclusions as events that we then have to deal with. We are, however, all free to decide how to react to whatever is presented to us at every moment of our lives.

Your destiny is linked directly with your personality because the choices you make, consciously or unconsciously, depend largely on your own natural inclinations. It is these inclinations that psychological astrology describes. You can live out every single part of your chart in a constructive or a less constructive way. For instance, if you have Aries strong in your chart, action and initiative will play a major role in your life. It is your choice whether you express yourself aggressively or assertively, heroically or selfishly, and also whether you are the doer or the done-to. Making the right choices is important because every decision has consequences – and what you give out, sooner or later, you get back. If you don't know and understand yourself, you are 'fated' to act according to instinct and how your life experiences have conditioned you. By revealing how you are wired up temperamentally, astrology can highlight alternatives to blind knee-jerk reactions, which often make existing problems worse. This self-knowledge can allow you to make more informed free-will choices, and so help you create a better and more successful future for yourself.

Astrology and Prediction

Astrology cannot predict specific events based on your birth chart. That kind of prediction belongs to clairvoyance and divination. These specialities, when practised by gifted and responsible individuals, can give penetrating insights into events that are likely to happen in the future if matters proceed along their present course.

The real benefit of seeing into the future is that if we don't like what could happen if we carry on the way we're going, we can take steps either to prevent it or to lessen its impact. Rarely is the future chiselled out in stone. There are many possible futures. What you feed with your attention grows. Using your birth chart, a competent astrologer can map out, for years in advance, major turning points, showing which areas of your life will be affected at these times and the kind of change that will be taking place. This information gives answers to the questions that most clients ask in one way or another: 'Why me, why this and why now?' If you accept responsibility for facing what needs to be done at the appropriate time, and doing it, you can change the course of your life for the better.

Astrology and the Soul

What is sometimes called the soul and its purpose is a mystery much more profound than astrology. Most of us have experienced 'chance' meetings and apparent 'tragedies' which have affected the direction of our entire lives. There is an intelligence at work that is infinitely wiser and more powerful than the will or wishes of our small egocentric personalities. This force, whatever name we give it – Universal Wisdom, the Inner Guide, the Self, a guardian angel – steers us into exactly the right conditions for our souls' growth. Astrology can pinpoint the turning points in the course of your destiny and describe the equipment that you have at your disposal for serving, or resisting, the soul's purpose. That equipment is your personality.

Who Are You?

You are no doubt aware of your many good qualities as well as your rather more resistible ones that you might prefer to keep firmly under wraps. Maybe you have wondered why it is that one part of your personality seems to want to do one thing while another part is stubbornly intent on doing the exact opposite. Have you ever wished that you could crack the code that holds the secrets of what makes you – and significant others – behave in the complex way you do? The good news is that you can, with the help of your astrological birth chart, sometimes known as your horoscope.

Just as surely as your DNA identifies you and distinguishes you from everyone else, as well as encoding your peculiarities and potential, your birth chart reveals the unique 'DNA fingerprinting' of your personality. This may seem a staggering claim, but it is one that those who have experienced serious astrology will endorse, so let's take a closer look at what a birth chart is.

Your Birth Chart

Your birth chart is a simplified diagram of the positions of the planets, as seen from the place of your birth, at the moment you took your first independent breath. Critics have said that astrology is obviously nonsense because birth charts are drawn up as if the Sun and all the planets moved round the Earth.

We know in our minds that the Earth moves round the Sun, but that doesn't stop us seeing the Sun rise in the east in the morning and move across the sky to set in the west in the evening. This is an optical illusion. In the same way, we know (or at least most of us know) that we are not really the centre of the universe, but that doesn't stop us experiencing ourselves as being at the focal point of our own personal worlds. It is impossible to live life in any other way. It is the strength, not weakness, of astrology that it describes from your own unique viewpoint how you, as an individual, experience life.

Erecting Your Chart

To draw up a full birth chart you need three pieces of information – the date, time and place of your birth. With your birth date alone you can find the positions of all the planets (except sometimes the Moon) to a good enough degree of accuracy to reveal a great deal of important information about you. If you have the time and place of birth, too, an astrologer can calculate your Ascendant or Rising Sign and the houses of your chart – see below. The Ascendant is a bit like the front door of your personality and describes your general outlook on life. (If you know your Ascendant sign, you might like to read more about its characteristics in the book on that sign in this series.)

The diagram on page 6 shows what a birth chart looks like. Most people find it pretty daunting at first sight but it actually breaks down into only four basic units – the planets, the signs, the aspects and the houses.

The Planets

Below is a simple list of what the planets represent.

PLANET	REPRESENTS YOUR URGE TO
☉ The Sun	express your identity
☽ The Moon	feel nurtured and safe
☿ Mercury	make connections
♀ Venus	attract what you love
♂ Mars	assert your will
♃ Jupiter	find meaning in life
♄ Saturn	achieve your ambitions
♅ Uranus	challenge tradition
♆ Neptune	serve an ideal
♇ Pluto	eliminate, transform and survive

The planets represent the main psychological drives that every single one of us has. The exact way in which we express these drives is not fixed from birth but develops and evolves throughout our lives, both consciously and unconsciously. In this book we will be examining in detail four of these planets – your Sun, Moon, Mercury and Venus. These are the bodies that are right at the heart of our solar system. They correspond, in psychological astrology, to the core of your personality and represent how you express yourself, what motivates you emotionally, how you use your mind and what brings you pleasure.

The Signs
The signs your planets are in show how you tend to express your inner drives. For example, if your Mars is in the action sign of Aries, you will assert yourself pretty directly, pulling no punches. If your Venus is in secretive Scorpio, you will attract, and also be attracted to, emotionally intense relationships. There is a summary of all of the signs on p. 128.

The Aspects
Aspects are important relationships between planets and whether your inner characteristics clash with or complement each other depends largely on whether or not they are in aspect and whether that aspect is an easy or a challenging one. In Chapter Six we'll be looking at some challenging aspects to the Sun.

The Houses
Your birth chart is divided into 12 slices, called houses, each of which is associated with a particular area of life, such as friendships, travel or home life. If, for example, you have your Uranus in the house of career, you are almost

certainly a bit of a maverick at work. If you have your Neptune in the house of partnership, you are likely to idealise your husband, wife or business partner.

The Nature of Time

Your birth chart records a moment in time and space, like a still from a movie – the movie being the apparent movement of the planets round the earth. We all know that time is something that can be measured in precise units, which are always the same, like seconds, months and centuries. But if you stop to reflect for a moment, you'll also recognise that time doesn't always feel the same. Twenty minutes waiting for a bus on a cold, rainy day can seem like a miserable eternity, while the same amount of time spent with someone you love can pass in a flash. As Einstein would say – that's relativity.

There are times in history when something significant seems to be in the air, but even when nothing momentous is happening the quality of time shifts into different 'moods' from moment to moment. Your birth chart is impregnated with the qualities of the time when you were born. For example, people who were born in the mid-to-late 1960s, when society was undergoing major disruptive changes, carry those powerful energies within them and their personalities reflect, in many ways, the turmoil of those troubled and exciting times. Now, as adults, the choices that those individuals make, based on their own inner conflicts and compulsions, will help shape the future of society for better or worse. And so it goes on through the generations.

Seed Meets Soil

There is no such thing as a good or bad chart, nor is any one sign better or worse than another. There are simply 12 different, but equally important, life focuses. It's useful to keep in mind the fact that the chart of each one of us is made up of all the signs of the zodiac. This means that we'll act out, or experience, *every* sign somewhere in our lives. It is true, however, that some individual charts are more challenging than others; but the greater the challenge, the greater the potential for achievement and self-understanding.

In gardening terms, your chart is a bit like the picture on a seed packet. It shows what you could become. If the seeds are of poppies, there's no way you'll get petunias, but external conditions will affect how they grow. With healthy soil, a friendly climate and green-fingered gardeners, the plants have an excellent chance of flourishing. With poor soil, a harsh climate or constant neglect, the seeds will be forced to struggle. This is not always a disadvantage. They can become hardy and adapt, finding new and creative ways of evolving and thriving under more extreme conditions than the plant that was well cared for. It's the same with your chart. The environment you were raised in may have been friendly or hostile to your nature and it will have done much to shape your life until now. Using the insights of astrology to affirm who you are, you can, as an adult, provide your own ideal conditions, become your own best gardener and live out more fully – and successfully – your own highest potential.

TWO

The Symbolism of Taurus

WE CAN LEARN A GREAT DEAL ABOUT TAURUS BY LOOKING at the symbolism and the myths and legends associated with it. These are time-honoured ways of describing psychological truths; they carry more information than plain facts alone and hint at the deeper meanings and significance of the sign.

The Taurus glyph of a circle with an upturned semicircle on top has been interpreted in many ways over the years and each interpretation helps build up a more complete picture of Taurean characteristics.

The most widespread and obvious one is that it resembles a bull's head and horns, drawing attention to the bull-like nature of Taurus. The bull is normally placid and happy to go about its own contented business of grazing and fertilising, but when goaded can go on the rampage and destroy.

The glyph can be seen too as the yoke that harnesses the massive power of the ox to plough fields and through slow, steady work turn the potential and raw materials of nature into food and riches.

It also suggests a wheel, referring both to the inventiveness of the Taurean brain in finding practical solutions to problems and to the Taurean capacity to carry heavy burdens uncomplainingly. In esoteric terms, it hints at the deep Taurean involvement and satisfaction with being incarnated on the wheel of life.

Two areas of the body associated with Taurus can also be seen pictured in the glyph. One is the womb and fallopian tubes, pointing to the sign's association with the pleasures of sex and fertility. The other is the neck and throat — the semi-circle is the jaw — which Taurus traditionally rules. Many Taureans have beautiful singing voices.

Perhaps the most poetic interpretation is to see the glyph as the graceful crescent Moon outstretched and open to receive life's treasures and abundance, balanced on top of the closed circle, representing both the full moon, pregnant with fertile life, and the circle of eternity, expressed through the individual.

Taurus the Bull

Although the symbol of Taurus is the very masculine figure of the bull, it is also associated with the ox and the cow. The cow from antiquity has represented docility, beauty, fertility and abundance and is, to this day, still a sacred beast in parts of Asia. The ox symbolises the Taurean themes of patience, strength, gentleness, work and wealth. In ancient religions the bull stood for the reproductive powers of nature, which is the source of all creation. The bull was revered in ancient Egypt. The rulers and later pharaohs gave themselves the title of The Bull and were often depicted in the form of that animal. The bull can also be a symbol of Mammon, the god of riches. While waiting for Moses to come down from

Mount Sinai, where he was receiving the Ten Commandments from God, the Israelites persuaded Moses' brother, Aaron, to make a bull-calf out of gold, which they then worshipped as a god. Moses was furious and destroyed it as a false idol. Some Taureans are in danger of falling into the trap of selling their souls to Mammon – worshipping outer wealth and worldly values – instead of appreciating those things that have higher and lasting value.

The Ruler of Taurus

Venus, or Aphrodite as she is known in Greek mythology, is the ruler of Taurus. She is a goddess completely devoid of shame around her sexuality and the pleasures of the senses. Never a victim or pushover, she knows what she wants and goes about getting it, allowing nothing and nobody to stand in her way. When her will is thwarted she is a dangerous enemy, but her favourites are rewarded with great generosity. She can also be lazy, vain and focused on her own desires, the downside of Taurus.

Taurus in Myth and Legend

Taurus is often thought to be a simple sign, easy to understand and with very little depth and few interests apart from money, food and sex. This is far from true. One myth that throws light on Taurean complexity, and on what happens when Taurus strays from the straight and narrow, is the story of King Minos and the minotaur. Minos and his two brothers all had claim to be King of Crete. Minos prayed to the god Poseidon to send a bull out of the sea as a sign that Minos was the rightful King and in return Minos promised to sacrifice the bull to Poseidon as a mark of thanks and respect. The bull was sent and Minos crowned, but Minos didn't honour his part of the bargain. Instead his greed got the better of him and he kept the fine bull for himself and sacrificed a substitute. As a punishment Poseidon had Aphrodite make the wife of Minos fall passionately in love with the bull. Out of this odd coupling was born the minotaur, a monster with a man's body and a bull's head, which fed off human flesh. Minos was mortified and had a vast labyrinth built to hide and imprison the beast. To repay a debt to Minos, the King of Athens was forced, every year, to send a group of young Athenians to be fed to the minotaur. This naturally did not go down well with the citizens of Athens. So one year Theseus, son of the king of Athens, volunteered to be among the sacrificial party. Ariadne, the daughter of Minos, decided to help him. She gave Theseus a ball of thread which he unravelled as he went in; with that to guide him, and after he had slain the minotaur, he was able to find his way out of the maze.

This story tells of how the desire to possess, or to hold on to what should be let go of, and the wilful refusal to do what the conscience knows is right, can lead to the unleashing of something monstrous and destructive in the lives of Taureans, something that may have grave consequences for many people. One of your major challenges as a Taurean is to put your considerable gifts for accumulating power and resources into serving the common wealth and not to be run by your intense desires and wilfulness. The ball of thread hints at a way out of this core Taurean problem, which is to find a way of making a connection between the outer world of everyday consciousness and the sometimes dark and convoluted inner world of your own hidden passions.

The Season of Taurus

It is no coincidence that the sign of Taurus falls, in the northern hemisphere where astrology originated, in the fullness of spring. This is the mating season, celebrated by the old Celtic fire festival of Beltane. It is also the time when the new life that stirred from its winter sleep and thrust itself out of the earth at the time of Aries bursts into full abundance and beauty, with further promise of a rich harvest to come.

THREE

The Heart of the Sun

THE GLYPH FOR THE SUN IS A PERFECT CIRCLE WITH A DOT in the centre and symbolises our dual nature — earthly and eternal. The circle stands for the boundary of the personality, which distinguishes and separates each individual from every other individual, for it is our differences from other people that make us unique, not our similarities. The dot in the centre indicates the mysterious 'divine spark' within us and the potential for becoming conscious of who we truly are, where we have come from and what we may become.

The Meaning of the Sun

Each of your planets represents a different strand of your personality. The Sun is often reckoned to be the most important factor of your whole birth chart. It describes your sense of identity, and the sign that the Sun was in when you were born, your Sun sign, along with its house position and any aspects to other planets, shows how you express and develop that identity.

Your Role in Life

Each of the signs is associated with certain roles that can be played in an infinite number of ways. Take one of the roles of Aries, which is the warrior. A warrior can cover anything from Attila the Hun, who devastated vast stretches of Europe with his deliberate violence, to an eco-warrior, battling to save the environment. The role, warrior, is the same; the motivation and actions are totally different. You can live out every part of your personality in four main ways – as creator, destroyer, onlooker or victim. How you act depends on who you choose to be from the endless variations possible from the symbolism of each of your planets, but most particularly your Sun. And you do have a choice; not all Geminis are irresponsible space cadets nor is every Scorpio a sex-crazed sadist. This book aims to paint a picture of what some of your choices might be and show what choices, conscious or unconscious, some well-known people of your sign have made.

Your upbringing will have helped shape what you believe about yourself and out of those beliefs comes, automatically, behaviour to match. For example, if you believe you are a victim, you will behave like one and the world will happily oblige by victimising you. If you see yourself as a carer, life will present you with plenty to care for – and often to care about, too. If you identify yourself as an adventurer, you'll spot opportunities at every corner. If you're a winner, then you'll tend to succeed. Shift the way that you see yourself and your whole world shifts, too.

Your Vocation

Your Sun describes your major life focus. This is not always a career. As the poet Milton said: 'They also serve who only stand and wait.' It is impossible to tell from your Sun sign exactly what your calling is – there are people of all signs occupied in practically every area of life. What is important is not so much *what* you do, but the way that you do it and it is this – how you express yourself – that your Sun describes. If you spend most of your time working at an occupation or living in a situation where you can't give expression to the qualities of your Sun, or which forces you to go against the grain of your Sun's natural inclinations, then you're likely to live a life of quiet, or possibly even noisy, desperation.

On Whose Authority

Your personality, which your birth chart maps, is like a sensitive instrument that will resonate only to certain frequencies – those that are similar to its own. Your Sun shows the kind of authority that will strike a chord with you, either positively or negatively, because it is in harmony with yours. It can show how you relate to people in authority, especially your father. (It is the Moon that usually shows the relationship with your mother and home.) In adult life it can throw light onto the types of bosses you are likely to come across, and also how you could react to them. It is a major part of the maturing process to take responsibility for expressing your own authority wisely. When you do so, many of your problems with external authorities diminish or even disappear.

In a woman's chart the Sun can also describe the kind of husband she chooses. This is partly because, traditionally, a husband had legal authority over his wife. It is also because, especially in the early years of a marriage, many women choose to pour their energies into homemaking and supporting their husbands' work in the world, rather than their own, and so his career becomes her career. As a

Taurean, you may find that your father, boss or husband shows either the positive or negative traits of Taurus or, as is usually the case, a mixture of both – calm, practical and contented or stubborn, controlling and dogmatic.

Born on the Cusp

If you were born near the beginning or end of Taurus, you may know that your birthday falls on the cusp, or meeting point, of two signs. The Sun, however, can only be in one sign or the other. You can find out for sure which sign your Sun is in by checking the tables on pp. 97–8.

FOUR

The Drama of Being a Taurus

EACH SIGN IS ASSOCIATED WITH A CLUSTER OF ROLES THAT HAVE their own core drama or storyline. Being born is a bit like arriving in the middle of an ongoing play and slipping into a certain part. How we play our characters is powerfully shaped in early life by having to respond to the input of the other actors around us – the people that make up our families and communities. As the play of our lives unfolds, we usually become aware that there are themes which tend to repeat themselves. We may ask ourselves questions like 'Why do I always end up with all the work / caught up in fights / with partners who mistreat me / in dead-end jobs / successful but unhappy . . .?'or whatever. Interestingly, I've found that people are less likely to question the wonderful things that happen to them again and again.

The good news is that once we recognise the way we have been playing our roles, we can then use our free-will choice to do some creative re-scripting, using the same character in more constructive scenarios. Even better news is that if we change, the other people in our dramas have got to make some alterations, too. If you refuse to respond to the same old cues in the customary ways, they are going to have to get creative too.

A core role of Taurus is the steward. A steward looks after the property or affairs of other people, as well as his or her own. Good stewards are scrupulously honest, completely trustworthy and aim to manage and protect wisely the affairs and resources entrusted to them, making the enterprise show some profit and growth wherever possible. Loving, cherishing and caring for what they have control over, they do not annex them as their own exclusive property. As they manage their estate prudently, in the fullness of time this can then be passed on to future generations. Understanding and accepting the difference between stewardship and ownership can be one of your major challenges as a Taurean. Taureans are the stewards of the world's resources — nature's material abundance and beauty — and the token that represents them. Money.

The parable of the talents has a tale to tell of Taurean stewardship at its finest and most miserly. A rich man, who had to go travelling, entrusted his goods to his three servants. He gave each of them, according to his ability, a number of coins, called talents. One was given five, another two and the last only one. The men who had been given five and two talents invested them wisely and doubled their money. The unfortunate who had been given only one, being over-cautious, buried his for safety. When the owner returned, he asked the servants how they had managed his money. He praised the two who had used their talents well and promoted them. The one who had, from fear, hoarded his was turfed out on his ear, minus cash. The message is clear: use it or lose it. As a cautious and shrewd Taurean, you have the green-finger potential for making all that you touch grow and flourish, whether this is plants, power, peace or pennies. Neglect these talents through fear, sloth or greed and you stand to lose out on the very things you hold dear.

Other roles associated with Taurus centre on working with and appreciating the earth's resources. They are the builder, gardener, farmer, caretaker, artist, artisan, conservationist, musician, gourmet and collector. Negative roles are the dictator and destroyer, where the inner demons of fear and greed, plus desire for control, overwhelm the personality and the once gentle and kindly bull sees red and turns dangerous.

The life of every Taurean is, at some stage, touched by a challenge or crisis concerning money or resources. For some it is loss, or threat of loss; for others it can be the equally unsettling experience of finding themselves in charge of plenty.

How you choose to see your role will determine your behaviour. The following chapter describes some typical Taurus behaviour. Remember, though, that there is no such thing as a person who is all Taurus and nothing but Taurus. You are much more complicated than that and other parts of your chart will modify, or may even seem to contradict, the single, but central, strand of your personality which is your Sun sign. These other sides of your nature will add colour and contrast and may restrict or reinforce your basic Taurus identity. They won't, however, cancel out the challenges you face as a Taurean.

FIVE

The Taurus Temperament

IT'S THE SIMPLE THINGS IN LIFE THAT BRING YOU CONTENTMENT. TO borrow from the beautiful words of Omar Khayyam, with a loaf of bread beneath the bough, a jug of wine, a book of verse – and a loved one beside you, singing (plus a home that you own, of course) – that's what you call paradise.

The Pleasures of the Senses

The pleasures of the senses delight you – the soft breath of wind on a summer's day, the rise and fall of birdsong, the majestic vibrancy of sunrise or sunset. Ancient, slow-growing trees and massive immovable mountains symbolise the peace you love so much. You have an appreciation of beauty that verges on reverence, whether it is of the natural or more cultivated human variety. Many Taureans have a good eye for harmony and colour and their stunning dress sense proves it. Others have little time for such vanities, preferring to go *au naturel*, and can look as though they have done their personal grooming with the aid of a pitchfork.

Your sense of touch is often highly developed and you

love to feel your skin in contact with the softness of silk and fur and satin. Sinking your fingers deep into sand or seed or soil brings you quiet but intense satisfaction. Touching and stroking something pleasing calms and soothes you when the stress levels rise. Male or female, you'll almost certainly respond to perfumed pleasures and even the most macho of Taurean men have been known to 'borrow' their partner's pampering preparations. Some even have their own well-stocked shelf or two in the bathroom.

Food, Glorious Food

It has been said that Taurean interests can be summed up in three words – money, food and sex – and there is some truth in that. When it comes to food, the typical Taurean prefers good, traditional, wholesome fare to messed-about fancy stuff. Many, however, are enthusiastic foodies and superb cooks. If you are one, even when dining alone you will go to great lengths to ensure that your table is spread with the finest. You don't mind forking out for the best of food and wine, but you abhor waste of any kind. Value for money is high on your list of priorities.

The Healing Power of Music

Most Taureans find inner peace through music of some sort, whether it is chants, jazz, rock or classical. Many are excellent musicians. The rhythmic quality of sound can help you express, and take the pressure off, the raw emotions and unprocessed thoughts held deep inside you, slowly building up pressure like a dormant volcano, trapped far beneath the earth's surface.

It is a rare Taurean that will dig down deep into the workings of the unconscious. Imagination is seldom your strong point, as you much prefer what is under your nose or in your hands. Some Taureans are, in fact, disinclined to believe in the reality of anything that they can't touch, taste, see or smell. Being completely at home in the world of objects, your reality is made up of things that have substance. The invisible or theoretical holds little appeal. You prefer to feel the earth beneath your feet and grit under your fingernails. If you are an exception to this rule, more than likely you'll have a powerful water or air component in your chart, as did Sigmund Freud, who had his Ascendant in Scorpio and Moon in Gemini.

Holding Firm to the Familiar

The reluctance to step out of a comfortable and accustomed rut is the downside of Taurean steadfastness of purpose. What's known and familiar pleases you best. Many Taureans are completely unadventurous and prefer to keep their legs solidly planted under their own tables and their heads on their own familiar pillows. I know one stay-at-home Taurean who was given a surprise free trip to Barbados by Concorde and practically had to be fork-lifted onto the plane, so great was his resistance. But once he got there and found it was to his liking – guess where he now returns to again and again?

Your task is to be an anchor and hold firm the centre of all that you do. It's essential, then, that you feel in control of situations to ensure that nothing changes too much, too quickly. Your aim is peace, predictability and stability and your impulse is to conserve, cherish and care for the goodness and goodies of the world. This is why so many Taureans have been notable peace-makers, practical carers and philanthropists, like Jean Henri Dunant, who helped found the Red Cross, and Bertrand Russell, who at the age of 89 was jailed for demonstrating against nuclear weapons using the favourite Taurean tactic of sitting down and refusing to budge. The downside, however, of the control factor is that, in insecure or emotionally damaged Taureans, it can go too far and begin to interfere with the freedom of others. The steps from keeping a firm guiding hand on the rudder to control freak to dictator are not large ones, especially if extensive power is involved. Some of the world's most notorious dictators have been Taureans, like Adolf Hitler, Pol Pot, Ayatollah Khomeini and Saddam Hussein.

What's Mine's Mine

Once you've found something that gives you pleasure and have decided to make it yours, you will not give up until that person or thing is in your possession for keeps. God help anybody who tries to get in your way, or to take it away from you. Taurean children are often reluctant to share their toys until they have taken over full possession of them and are absolutely sure that they will get them back. Taurean adults usually aren't so very different.

It is this intensity of desire, coupled with an inflexible will of iron, which causes the worst of Taurean problems. When Taureans say 'I can't change' they aren't just being difficult – they are simply stating how it is for them. Inertia is your middle name. You can be cautious to the point of catatonic but once you've gathered momentum, got up a head of steam and set your course to steady, you can feel it's almost impossible to swerve on to another track. Stand in the way of a bull when it is pounding at full tilt toward its objective and the result is total devastation. Frustration of a powerful will, fixity of intention, in-built difficulties with processing feelings and the ability to justify any actions that will result in gaining control can sometimes lead to violence. Tragically – if several other chart factors point in that direction too – this can occasionally be extreme, as in the cases of Thomas Hamilton, who gunned down a class of young schoolchildren and then shot himself because he was being thwarted in his attempts to work with youth groups. Cult leader Jim Jones also killed himself along with 914 of his followers in Guyana in 1978 when he was threatened with exposure. Fortunately for the world, the overwhelming majority of Taureans are firmly on the side of the angels, with limitless supplies of patience, devotion, grace and gentleness.

Give Me Money

Most Taureans have a special gift, which is practically a Midas touch, for attracting money and possessions. These are symbols of your own power in the world. If you come across Taureans who are poor, in either property or artistic gifts, they are likely to be blocked off for some reason from their Sun's full potential. Energy has got to go somewhere, so look at their close associates and you're almost certain to find somebody else hogging control – or the purse strings.

Many Taureans are avid collectors. You can have superb taste that is usually fairly traditional, furnishing your home with the finest of carpets, paintings and furniture. You may, on the other hand, just accumulate. One Taurean I know was fascinated with the idea of feng shui and space-clearing but always pulled back from taking the first step. I suggested that she start with something relatively easy, like her underwear. She opened the first drawer, rifled through it nervously, picking up one greying, saggy-elasticated, two-sizes-too-small, limp piece of lingerie after the other. I held out the rubbish bin encouragingly. 'But these might come in useful one day,' she wailed, and shut the drawer firmly. She eventually parted, reluctantly, with the most battle-worn of her undergarments. But that was only after much coaxing, a glass or two of wine and – this is what clinched the deal – the promise that much more abundance would flow into her drawers if only she cleared out the compost.

One Thing at a Time

Like all of the earth signs, you have a special relationship with time. You like to have plenty of it. If anybody tries to rush you, you're likely to slow down even more, partly just to be awkward but also to give you time to assess the situation. Like a cow chewing cud, you'll ruminate over matters. When, eventually, you've made up your mind, you'll move at the appropriate pace – usually slow, measured and leisurely – towards whatever endpoint you've decided on. And, unless you have lot of fire in your chart, it will be a realistic, achievable goal. Pie-in-the-sky dreams are not for you. You like to prepare the ground carefully, sift over everything and, like a gardener, work out carefully what, if anything, will grow in the given climate or soil.

Your rhythm is attuned to the slow but regular cycles of nature, to the rise of the sap in spring and the fall of the leaves in autumn. It is not entirely true that Taureans hate change. You love the slow shift of the seasons, the constant procession of new wonders to be savoured. Change at that pace you not only welcome – you positively relish it. As Taurean poet Robert Browning wrote:

> The lark's on the wing;
> The snail's on the thorn;
> God's in His heaven –
> All's right with the world!

All Change

What leaves you completely rattled is uncertainty and sudden, unpredictable change. When those threaten, or happen, you go into a frozen state, not moving either physically or emotionally until you have, cautiously and slowly, made some kind of sense of the pattern. Then, having come to your conclusions, you will move, often abruptly and always with finality, changing your thinking, behaviour or circumstances, and become just as attached to the new order as you were to the phase before.

Believe You Me

Complexity puzzles and often irritates you. You are a great fan of the acronym K.I.S.S. – Keep It Simple, Sweetie. For this reason, many Taureans who are religiously, philosophically or politically inclined can have a dogmatic certainty about the rightness of their way. Some can even be downright rude, hostile and offensive about anybody else's point of view. C.G. Jung, Freud's most famous protégé, broke off with him because Freud refused to consider Jung's differing views or to let go of the reins of control in the relationship. Religious Taureans are often drawn to traditional ceremonial rituals, especially sacred song or dance, which soothe and comfort them. Non-religious ones, like Karl Marx, can brandish their theories with all the fervour of an evangelical preacher.

Taurus at Work

Financial security matters to you, so a predictable monthly pay cheque, a guaranteed pension and the chance of regular promotions are right up your street. Thanks to your practical common sense, you are good at tasks that need patience and persistence. You prefer to work at an unhurried pace and do a job thoroughly. Once you've grasped the basics, you'll throw your time and energy into achieving results. As you are rarely interested in hogging the limelight, you'll happily work behind the scenes in supportive and advisory roles, being a pillar of strength in times of crisis. You're generally scrupulously honest, loyal and dependable so often end up in positions of trust. You much prefer to be boss of your own domain but you'll happily knuckle down and take orders until you finally reach that position. You are in no hurry to go anywhere fast but you are quietly ambitious, and if there is no chance of promotion in your current job, you'll move on to somewhere there is. A job in the country would be ideal, but you'll be contented in town if your fellow workers are co-operative and the work environment is peaceful.

Financial Wizardry

With your excellent business sense, knack of making money and healthy scepticism about innovative schemes and wild investments, you could do well in such areas as accountancy, investment banking and financial and political administration. Anything that requires enterprise, razzmatazz or snap character assessments is probably best left to someone else. With your down-to-earth bluntness and your tendency to blow raspberries at pretension, your salesmanship potential – except for property and finance – could have its limitations, unless, of course, your chart has a strong Gemini influence. Then, with your persistence and patter, you could sell snow to Siberia and sand in the Sahara.

Many Taureans are drawn to musical careers as singers, performers or composers. Gardening or farming may be good choices too. Being gifted at crafting raw materials into something of value, building, engineering, sculpture, pottery, antiques and furniture-making could have an appeal. With your love of colour and form, working in the visual arts as an artist, sculptor, designer or illustrator are often good options, as well as jobs in the beauty business.

Taurus and Health

Taureans tend to be comfortable with their bodies and generally have cast iron digestions and plenty of stamina, so much so that you can push yourself to the limits before taking a rest. This is rarely a wise move. It's important that you establish healthy habits early on, because you'll find it difficult to change once they're firmly entrenched.

Taurean energy is retentive so your body tends to hold on to whatever goes into it. Long walks in the country, heavy-duty gardening, or building with stone might suit your exercise programme. Without pumping some iron, your slow approach to life plus love of good grub can soon have the pounds piling on and undermining what should be a healthy constitution. You probably don't need reminding that sex is a wonderful work-out, too (though when I mentioned to a Taurean friend that the calorie input/ output figures for sticky toffee pudding and a wild night of passion do not balance out, she accused me of peddling dodgy maths and said she'd take her chances).

Taurus rules the throat, vocal cords and the thyroid. When you're under stress or insecure, it's in these areas that problems could arise – or in the reproductive organs, heart or bowels. If the thyroid becomes underactive, you'll be even more sluggish than usual, as the thyroid rules the metabolism. If it's overactive, it can lead to anxiety and nervous tension, interfering with your need for peace, inner as well as outer.

Taurus in Love

For you, creating a relationship is like building a wall. One stone or experience is placed on another, checking that it will hold out against time and the elements. Familiarity may breed contempt with other signs, but not with Taurus. You love what's familiar and prefer old friends to new. Sometimes you can be slow off the mark in initiating romance and may even prefer the other to do the running. Periods of silence, as well as time on your own, are essential for your well-being. You need to have the sense from people in your life that you're free to potter around, preferably in the country or a garden, lost in contented contemplation of your surroundings.

Fatal Attractions

You've a great deal to offer to any relationship – loyal support and patience, a robust sense of humour and utter reliability. As you can be counted on to deal, without fuss, with any practical problems, you are a tower of strength in times of trouble. You're more than likely to be solvent and you don't see the point in playing mind games. With you, what you see is what you get and you'd probably prefer your partner to be every bit as straightforward. Life being the way it is, however, you've a powerful attraction to those who're wildly different from you. Your need for security can lead to a mistrust that can verge on the phobic about spontaneity, drama, rashness and the irrational. Yet these are the very qualities that you are so often drawn to in a partner. So many Taureans are magnetically pulled to partners whose charts have important planets in the fire signs – Aries, Leo and Sagittarius. Relationships like these can work beautifully, if you're both prepared to make a few necessary adjustments to your expectations, as you complement each other so well.

Dealing with Differences

You tend to accept people and situations unquestioningly, as a simple fact of life. If they don't interfere with you, you won't interfere with them. The first signs of trouble you'll tend to ignore, hoping the problem will just go away. If it doesn't, you'll either pretend it's not happening or make the odd grumpy comment but nothing much will show on the surface. If the irritant persists long enough and strong enough, eventually you'll act – decisively and possibly explosively. Listening to your partner at the beginning, and talking things over, could often prevent small problems building up into major dramas.

Even in the best of circumstances, it is sometimes hard for you to find the words to say that you care, so you let your gifts speak for you. When you're in love, you're attentive and helpful, showing your feelings by practical actions and tender little offerings rather than grand gestures and declarations of passion.

Taurus and Sex

A romantic relationship is on the rocks with you if sex is rationed. Pleasures of the flesh are essential for your well-being. If the sex is good, you will tend to hold on in there and come back for more, even if other parts of the relationship are shaky. All of your senses come into play in love-making. You're highly tactile, savouring skin brushing on skin and the natural scents of a lover's body drive you crazy with desire. You often prefer your thrills without frills and being a creature of habit you can sometimes get stuck in a sexual rut. Unless you are with a partner who prizes predictability, this may benefit from a little attention.

Taurus and Marriage

Since you value what is lasting, you need to be convinced that any partner is going to stick around before signing up for the long haul. Without that guarantee, for you, it's not a worthwhile emotional investment. Many Taureans marry late, if at all. It may seem odd at first that a sign so much in need of stability should be so slow to tie the knot. But taking a risk is hard for you and the idea of possible abandonment is terrifying, as, without continuity, the bottom would fall out of your world. You want to make sure that you've found the right person because, once you commit, you intend to stay forever. Divorce is a bitter pill for you to swallow and you'd usually prefer to stay in a situation that has soured and curdled rather than cut the ties that bind. However, if you judge the situation is beyond repair or redemption, you will resolutely turn your back on it and that is that. Finished. Full stop. Dialogue over. Next chapter, please.

SIX

Aspects of the Sun

PLANETS, JUST LIKE PEOPLE, CAN HAVE IMPORTANT RELATIONSHIPS with each other. These relationships are called aspects. Aspects to your Sun from any other planet can influence your personality markedly. The most powerful effects come with those from the slower-moving planets – Saturn, Uranus, Neptune or Pluto. Sometimes they can alter your ideas about yourself and your behaviour patterns so much that you may not feel at all typical of your sign in certain areas of your life.

Check if your birth date and year appear in the various sections below to find out if one or more of these planets was aspecting the Sun when you were born. Only the so-called challenging aspects have been included. These are formed when the planets are together, opposite or at right angles to each other in the sky.

Unfortunately, because space is restricted, other aspects have been left out, although they have similar effects to those described below and, for the same reason, a few dates will inevitably have been missed out, too. (You can find out for sure whether or not your Sun is aspected at my website www.janeridderpatrick.com) If your Sun has no aspects to Saturn, Uranus, Neptune or Pluto, you're more likely to be a typical Taurean.

Some well-known Taureans with challenging aspects to their Suns appear below. You can find more in the birthday section at the end of the book.

Taurus Sun in Aspect with Saturn

If you were born between 1940 and 1942, 1969 and 1971 or 1999 and 2000, whether or not your birthday is listed below, you are likely to feel the influence of Saturn on your Sun.

19–30 April in: 1932, 1939–40, 1947, 1954, 1961–2, 1969–70, 1976–7, 1983–4 and 1991

1–10 May in: 1933, 1941, 1948, 1955, 1962–3, 1970, 1977, 1984 and 1992

11–20 May in: 1942, 1949, 1956, 1963–4, 1971–2, 1978, 1985 and 1992–3

David Attenborough	Salvador Dalí	Margot Fonteyn
Walter de la Mare	Eva Perón	Donatella Versace

Wherever Saturn is around there is a powerful drive to prove yourself by your achievements and be endorsed by the rubber stamp of official recognition. Side by side with this ambition comes the fear of being found inadequate and disapproved of. Like everything else in the personality, you can work with this constructively or destructively. It is likely that in childhood you had some humiliating experiences of being overlooked, put down or shamed for not living up to somebody else's expectations, often your father's. If you still believe, as an adult, that you are controlled by some authority figure 'out there' who is judging you and holding you back, you can become stubbornly uncooperative and oversensitive to criticism. Not surprisingly, those same authorities are likely to be somewhat reluctant to help, promote or accept you. Another possibility is that you drip feed yourself so much criticism and negativity around your own worth and abilities that you simply stop trying and end up bitter and frustrated. If, however, you are willing to play by Saturn's rules, the result is very different. You can achieve lasting success and contentment, financial independence and a highly respected position in the world – all of the things for which your ambitions burn.

And Saturn's price? To identify clear, long-term goals in an area that touches your heart, not what you think you 'should' do. To listen to your inner critic when it speaks wisely, and silence it when it puts you down. To discipline yourself to do what you know is right and keep on keeping on. The world and all that's in it can be yours at the cost of a little constant effort. The poet Walter de la Mare worked for years in the accounts department of an oil company and ended up with a knighthood and – the ultimate accolade – being buried in St Paul's Cathedral. Just remember to stop frequently to smell the flowers and enjoy the day ...

Taurus Sun in Aspect with Uranus

19–30 April in: 1934–8, 1956–60, 1975–80 and 1995–9
1–10 May in: 1937–41, 1958–62, 1977–80 and 1997–2000
11–20 May in: 1939–43, 1960–63, 1978–82 and 1999–2000

Sigmund Freud	Shirley MacLaine	Guglielmo Marconi
Jack Nicholson	Robert Owen	Michelle Pfeiffer

Having a steadfast, and often stubborn, Taurus Sun in aspect with Uranus, the unpredictable, can lead to inner tension. Taurus needs stability, Uranus demands change. Because of this, you may often feel torn between two extremes, finding peace hard to come by. Something inside drives you to challenge the authorities or traditions of whatever system you find yourself in, whether it is a family, a company, institution or profession. Injustice or outworn attitudes in urgent need of improvement tend to grab your attention and you are rarely short of ideas for putting the matter to rights. At worst, you can be downright bloody-minded and doggedly contrary, refusing to consider that anybody else's opinions could possibly be right. At best, you are a public-spirited idealist who is willing and courageous enough to throw yourself into improving the human condition, no matter how long it takes. Reformer Robert Owen is an outstanding example. In the darkest days of industrial exploitation he built the model village of New Lanark in Scotland, with outstanding amenities for his own mill-workers, and this became the cradle of the cooperative movement.

Sun Uranus is the aspect of the rebel, the outsider – and the inventor. Marconi, undeterred by the scepticism of traditional scientists, demonstrated the potential of wireless waves by transmitting the first radio message across the Atlantic. You tend to be ahead of your time and the ideas and solutions that seem so blindingly obvious to you could initially meet with opposition, only to become part of mainstream thinking a few years down the line. A well-paid, exciting job offering plenty of fresh challenges is ideal for you. Women with this aspect often prefer partners who give them plenty of physical and emotional space.

Taurus Sun in Aspect with Neptune

19–30 April in: 1956–62
1–10 May in: 1960–8
11–20 May in: 1964–73

Cate Blanchett	Daniel Day-Lewis	Linda Evangelista
Yehudi Menuhin	Eva Perón	Tony Hancock

You can be acutely sensitive to both beauty and suffering; you'd love to capture the elusiveness of the first and to help alleviate the latter. You're likely to be a bit of a dreamer and may find hard reality painful or unappealing. Daniel Day-Lewis describes himself as a 'lifelong study of evasion'. You are happiest when you find an ideal to which you can dedicate your energies. For many, that is through selfless service or spirituality. For others, like Yehudi Menuhin, it is music. He set up a school to help young, talented musicians. Sun–Neptune can be a superb combination if you are involved in creative work, such as art, music, film or advertising because you have an uncanny knack of tuning in to people's desires and fantasies and finding ways of catering for or expressing them, often before they have become aware of these themselves. The legendary Eva Perón was seen by many Argentinians as a saint who loved the common people – others saw her as a gold-digger and creator of her own myth.

Some with this aspect have vague feelings of being flawed or unworthy or that they are victims of life's unfairness. They may then rely on a boss, partner or father figure to shore up their confidence. Others, especially women, may choose partners who are either unavailable, emotionally damaged or who need looking after or fixing. This may suit you perfectly but if it doesn't, there is no need to stay stuck, unless you take pleasure in being a martyr. It may feel difficult, even impossible, to disentangle yourself and move on to find a worthier cause into which you can pour your gentle, loving energies – but you can do it. You may need to learn to say no – firmly – as you tend to take on far too much because you feel guilty and over-responsible. When the going gets rough, though, do be careful not to fall into the temptation of trying to lose yourself in food or, like Tony Hancock did, in alcohol.

Taurus Sun in Aspect with Pluto

19–30 April in: 1938–49 and 1983–9
1–10 May in: 1946–55 and 1987–92
11–20 May in: 1951–9 and 1990–7

Tony Blair	Sid Vicious	Joanna Lumley
Jeremy Paxman	Barbra Streisand	David Suchet

It's not easy for you to trust. There can be a deep-seated suspicion that's hard to shake off, that something dangerous lurks round every corner. You like to have everything under your control, otherwise who knows what might happen. Some people might call you a control freak, and if you aren't, then the chances are that your father, boss or partner is. Some people with this aspect can have a sense of being unwanted or that there is something 'bad' or unacceptable about them. Others see evil 'out there' and are determined to destroy it. Power is always an issue for you. Your challenge is to use it wisely, to scrutinise your own motivations so that you can free yourself from fear and transform your world for the better by standing up to hypocrisy, corruption and the abuse of power.

Nobody could ever accuse you of a lack of drive. When

you make up your mind to push something through, you will keep at it no matter what the odds. Tony Blair pushed through Britain's participation in the Iraq War despite vociferous public anger and opposition. Your determination is formidable and you can drive yourself to breaking point and collapse, exhausted. You may have to be careful not to put people's backs up and get yourself, quite unintentionally, into unnecessary power struggles. Your work may take you into areas dealing with sex, secrets, research, death, large amounts of money – though not necessarily your own (sorry!) – or personal or political power.

You're probably rather secretive and defensive, feeling the need to protect yourself against your own vulnerability, emotional as well as physical. It may take you a long time before you can feel safe enough to show your true self, even to people close to you. Lowering your barriers occasionally – in a safe space – could radically improve your life.

SEVEN

Meeting Your Moon

☽ THE GLYPH FOR THE MOON IS THE SEMI-CIRCLE OR CRESCENT. It is a symbol for the receptiveness of the soul and is associated with feminine energies and the ebb and flow of the rhythms of life. In some Islamic traditions it represents the gateway to paradise and the realms of bliss.

The Sun and Moon are the two complementary poles of your personality, like yang and yin, masculine and feminine, active and reflective, career and home, father and mother. The Moon comes into its own as a guide at night, the time of sleeping consciousness. It also has a powerful effect on the waters of the earth. Likewise, the Moon in your birth chart describes what you respond to instinctively and feel 'in your waters', often just below the level of consciousness. It is your private radar system, sending you messages via your body responses and feelings, telling you whether a situation seems safe or scary, nice or nasty. Feelings provide vital information about circumstances in and around you. Ignore them at your peril; that will lead you into emotional, and sometimes even physical, danger. Eating disorders tend to be associated with being out of touch with, or neglecting, the instincts and the body, both of which the Moon describes.

Extraordinary though it might seem to those who are emotionally tuned in, some people have great difficulty in knowing what they are feeling. One simple way is to pay attention to your body. Notice any sensations that attract your attention. Those are linked to your feelings. Now get a sense of whether they are pleasant or unpleasant, then try to put a more exact name to what those feelings might be. Is it sadness, happiness, fear? What is it that they are trying to tell you? Your Moon hints at what will strongly activate your feelings. Learning to trust and decode this information will help make the world seem – and be – a safer place.

The Moon represents your drive to nurture and protect yourself and others. Its sign, house and aspects describe how you respond and adapt emotionally to situations and what feeds you, in every sense of the word. It gives information about your home and home life and how you experienced your mother, family and childhood, as well as describing your comfort zone of what feels familiar – the words 'family' and 'familiar' come from the same source. It shows, too, what makes you feel secure and what could comfort you when you're feeling anxious. Your Moon describes what moves and motivates you powerfully at the deepest instinctual level and indicates what is truly the 'matter' in – or with – your life.

Knowing children's Moon signs can help parents and teachers better understand their insecurities and respect their emotional make-up and needs, and so prevent unnecessary hurt, or even harm, to sensitive young lives. It's all too easy to expect that our children and parents should have the same emotional wiring as we do, but that's rarely how life works. Finding our parents' Moon signs can be a real revelation. It can often help us understand where they are coming from, what they need and why they react to us in the way they do. Many of my clients have been able to find the understanding and compassion to forgive their parents when they realised that they were doing their very best with the emotional resources available to them.

In relationships it is important that your Moon's requirements are met to a good enough extent. For example, if you have your Moon in Sagittarius you must have adventure, freedom and the opportunity to express your beliefs. If being with your partner constantly violates these basic needs, you will never feel secure and loved and the relationship could, in the long term, undermine you. However, if your Moon feels too comfortable, you will never change and grow. The art is to get a good working balance between support and challenge.

A man's Moon sign can show some of the qualities he will unconsciously select in a wife or partner. Some of the others are shown in his Venus sign. Many women can seem much more like their Moon signs than their Sun signs, especially if they are involved in mothering a family and being a support system for their husbands or partners. It is only at the mid-life crisis that many women start to identify more with the qualities of their own Suns rather than living that out through their partners' ambitions. Similarly, men tend to live out the characteristics of their Moon signs through their wives and partners until mid-life, often quite cut off from their own feelings and emotional responses. If a man doesn't seem at all like his Moon sign, then check out the women in his life. There's a good chance that his wife, mother or daughter will show these qualities.

Your Moon can be in any sign, including the same one as your Sun. Each sign belongs to one of the four elements: Fire, Earth, Air or Water. The element of your Moon can give you a general idea of how you respond to new situations and what you need to feel safe and comforted. We all become anxious if our Moon's needs are not being recognised and attended to. We then, automatically, go into our personal little rituals for making ourselves feel better. Whenever you are feeling distressed, especially when you are way out of your comfort zone in an unfamiliar situation, do something to feed and soothe your Moon. You're almost certain to calm down quickly.

Fire Moons

If you have a fire Moon in Aries, Leo or Sagittarius, your first response to any situation is to investigate in your imagination the possibilities for drama, excitement and self-expression. Feeling trapped by dreary routine in an ordinary humdrum life crushes you completely. Knowing that you are carrying out a special mission feeds your soul. To you, all the world's a stage and a voyage of discovery. Unless you are at the centre of the action playing some meaningful role, anxiety and depression can set in. To feel secure, you have to have an appropriate outlet for expressing your spontaneity, honourable instincts and passionate need to be of unique significance. The acknowledgement, appreciation and feedback of people around you are essential, or you don't feel real. Not to be seen and appreciated, or to be overlooked, can feel like a threat to your very existence.

Earth Moons

If you have an earth Moon in Taurus, Virgo or Capricorn, you'll respond to new situations cautiously and practically. Rapidly changing circumstances where you feel swept along and out of control are hard for you to cope with. You need time for impressions to sink in. Sometimes it is only much later, after an event has taken place, that you become sure what you felt about it. Your security lies in slowing down, following familiar routines and rituals, even if they are a bit obsessive, and focusing on something, preferably material – possibly the body itself or nature – which is comforting because it is still there. Indulging the senses in some way often helps too, through food, sex or body care. So does taking charge of the practicalities of the immediate situation, even if this is only mixing the drinks or passing out clipboards. To feel secure, you need continuity and a sense that you have your hand on the rudder of your own life. Think of the rather irreverent joke about the man seeming to cross himself in a crisis, all the while actually touching his most valued possessions to check that they are still intact – spectacles, testicles, wallet and watch. That must have been thought up by someone with the Moon in an earth sign.

Air Moons

When your Moon is in an air sign – Gemini, Libra or Aquarius – you feel most secure when you can stand back from situations and observe them from a distance. Too much intimacy chokes you and you'll tend to escape it by going into your head to the safety of ideas and analysis. Even in close relationships you need your mental, and preferably physical, space. You often have to think, talk or write about what you are feeling before you are sure what your feelings are. By putting them 'out there' so that you can examine them clearly, you can claim them as your own. Unfairness and unethical behaviour can upset you badly and make you feel uneasy until you have done something about it or responded in some way. It can be easy with an air Moon to be unaware of, or to ignore, your own feelings because you are more responsive to ideas, people and situations outside of yourself that may seem to have little connection with you. This is not a good idea, as it cuts you off from the needs of your body as well as your own emotional intelligence. Making opportunities to talk, play with and exchange ideas and information can reduce the stress levels if anxiety strikes.

Water Moons

Finally, if your Moon is in a water sign – Cancer, Scorpio or Pisces – you are ultra-sensitive to atmospheres, and you can experience other people's pain or distress as if they were your own. You tend to take everything personally and, even if the situation has nothing at all to do with you, feel responsible for making it better. Your worst nightmare is to feel no emotional response coming back from other people. That activates your deep-seated terror of abandonment, which can make you feel that you don't exist and is, quite literally, what you fear even more than death. If you feel insecure, you may be tempted to resort to emotional manipulation to try to force intimacy with others – not a good idea, as this can lead to the very rejection that you dread. You are at your most secure when the emotional climate is positive and you have trusted, supportive folk around who will winkle you out of hiding if you become too reclusive. With a water Moon, it is vital to learn to value your own feelings and to take them seriously – and to have a safe, private place you can retreat to when you feel emotionally fragile. As you never forget anything which has made a feeling impression on you, sometimes your reactions are triggered by unconscious memories of things long past, rather than what is taking place in the present. When you learn to interpret them correctly, your feelings are your finest ally and will serve you well.

Finding Your Moon Sign

If you don't yet know your Moon sign, before looking it up, you could have some fun reading through the descriptions that follow and seeing if you can guess which one it is. To find your Moon sign, check your year and date of birth in the tables on pp. 99–112. For a greater in-depth understanding of your Moon sign you might like to read about its characteristics in the book in this series about that sign.

At the beginning of each section are the names of some well-known Taureans with that particular Moon sign. You can find more about them in Chapter Ten.

Taurus Sun with Moon in Aries

Susan Atkins   Lucrezia Borgia   Robert Browning
Salvador Dalí   Jim Jones   Denis Thatcher

Your view of life is pretty straightforward. You want what you want when you want it and you can become intensely frustrated if anyone tries to stand in your way. With your fierce determination and intense desires, when you have made up your mind to do or have something, you can more or less count it as done. Your unshakeable belief in your own projects can make you an inspiring leader and a force to be reckoned with. You make a brilliant entrepreneur too, combining shrewd business sense and awesome promotional skills. At home you're likely to be on the go constantly, putting enormous amounts of energy into creating a secure, solid and comfortable base for yourself and your family. With your strong independent streak, you can't bear being told what to do. You much prefer to be in the driving seat and in total control in every situation, and are quite prepared to battle for that position. A man's Moon sign can often describe his wife — perhaps Denis Thatcher, husband of strong-willed Lady Thatcher, is a case in point.

Since your natural instincts are focused primarily on instantly following your own impulses and wants, in your rush to look after *numero uno* and push your agenda through, you may fail to notice or, in extreme cases, even bulldoze over the less self-assured, causing a huge build-up of resentment. It's easy to overlook this tendency or sweep it aside as unimportant because self-searching, or analysing complex emotional situations, doesn't come easily to you — unless other chart factors indicate differently. Your major challenge is to pay attention to other people and be considerate of their needs too. Every effort in that direction will pay off handsomely in the goodwill gained.

Taurus Sun with Moon in Taurus

Katharine Hepburn	Joanna Lumley	Karl Marx
Florence Nightingale	Robert Owen	Sheila Scott

Your practical and common-sense approach to whatever life throws at you makes you a dependable rock for everyone around. Like a still pool of peace, your presence is calming and reassuring. 'Where there's a will there's a way' is your motto. And what a formidable will you have too! Quietly and steadily, you will plod away doggedly until you have achieved whatever you've set your heart on, dealing with one obstacle after another as they come along until all resistance is worn down. As a young single woman, Florence Nightingale was up against formidable odds when she decided, in Victorian times, to follow her calling to run an army hospital. But the odds were less formidable than the indomitable Miss Nightingale. Florence had her way and the rest is history.

The material and sensual pleasures of life mean a lot to you – food, money, beauty, music and art. It's best to ask you for favours after a good meal and not before. You are probably a country person at heart, in love with the changing seasons and rhythms of nature. Intolerant of anything that doesn't agree with your world-view, you can be staggeringly dogmatic at times. Events you can't predict or control or that move too fast can unsettle you, and you may try to ignore or ridicule them away. However, things don't just vanish because you look the other way. From time to time your unprocessed feelings will erupt, leaving you, and anyone within earshot, reeling. If you deal with irritations as they arise instead of going for peace at any price, matters won't have to build up to this level and you'll find that more frequent minor confrontations mean real peace in the long-term.

Taurus Sun with Moon in Gemini

Sigmund Freud	Sid James	Daphne du Maurier
Edward Lear	Shirley Temple	Catherine the Great

With your needle-sharp responses and sparkling wit, you are a million miles away from the familiar strong, silent type of Taureans who bottle up their feelings and communicate in grunts. You are fascinated by just about everything, for a short time at least, and with your smooth-talking tongue can be a thorough charmer. It's rare for someone with this combination to be a party pooper. Most are socially active and you can be a great flirt. You've a low boredom threshold, a powerful curiosity and love bringing people together – and making deals.

Words fascinate you and you'll probably enjoy playing with them. Some, like Edward Lear, with his quirky nonsense verse, have turned this into an art form. Puns delight you and so does clever, earthy humour. It is often only by writing or talking about them that you find out what your feelings actually are. Freud spotted this, possibly from personal experience; a Freudian slip is where someone means to say one thing but comes out with something quite different, revealing what that person really feels, unconsciously, about the matter in hand.

You're skilled at lightning-quick analysis and putting two and two together to come up with brilliant new solutions to practical problems. Even experienced spin-doctors could learn a thing or two from you. You can use your clever tongue to gain, or keep, control of situations and you do love to have the last word. Your challenge is to find some balance between your urge to create peace and stability in your life, and an equally pressing desire for variety and change. Learning to hold on to your own personal truth and not be pulled off-centre by the bombardment of fascinating distractions around you is a skill worth acquiring.

Taurus Sun with Moon in Cancer

Bing Crosby	Penélope Cruz	Sandra Dee
Gabriel Fauré	Daniela Nardini	Benjamin Spock

Underneath that tower-of-strength exterior you are likely to be more sensitive than you care to admit, even to yourself. Being highly intuitive, you can pick up on atmospheres instantly and respond to them – a great asset for those who work with the public. Dr Benjamin Spock's common-sense manual *Baby and Child Care* advised parents to trust their own instincts. You feel deeply and are easily moved to tears, something men with this combination may try to suppress ruthlessly. It's easy for you to take other people's withdrawals and sulks personally even if they've nothing at all to do with you. Your fear of humiliation and rejection can make you cynical in self-protection. It's essential to find some way of expressing or discharging your feelings of resentment quickly or they can turn inward and eat away at you. Long walks in the country and music with a powerful rhythm can help you do that.

You are gentle, kind and helpful to anyone vulnerable or in need of care and protection. What is familiar is what feels safe and, man or woman, you may choose a partner you can mother or be mothered by. If you feel insecure, you can stay at home, refusing to budge, and can only be enticed out – pushing will just make you dig your heels in more firmly – by pleas for help or by the lure of serious sensual pleasures. Sex and financial security are vital to your well-being and you have an excellent, if cautious, business sense. Being so independent, it could be best for you to be in business by yourself or with those you consider family. Though you would cringe with embarrassment if you had to show it, you need appreciation like a flower needs rain. Why not just accept it graciously whenever it is offered?

Taurus Sun with Moon in Leo

Queen Elizabeth II	Brian Eno	Tony Hancock
Eva Perón	Barbra Streisand	Victoria Wood

Even if you seem quiet and gentle, you're a natural leader, with formidable organising skills. Some with this combination can be a touch bossy in their unquestioning belief in their right to be in charge and you've a happy knack of getting your own way. Being so focused on your own emotional dramas and thrown off-balance when people don't respond to them, you may, unintentionally, fail to notice the needs of others. Although being overlooked is your worst nightmare, your challenge is to learn to consider and respect the feelings of those around you too. This will bring you a double advantage: you will have their full attention, which is what you love, and you'll also feel good about yourself, because acting with generosity, honour and integrity is like food and drink to you. With your Moon in the royal sign of Leo, your highest function is to serve the people who give you the central role. The Queen exemplifies this combination at its finest. On her twenty-first birthday she made a solemn promise that she has never broken: 'I declare before you all, that my whole life, whether it be long or short, shall be devoted to your service . . .'.

You probably adore dressing-up and being made a fuss of. You expect the finest and usually get it and you could also be highly creative and a gifted performer, on or off a stage. As you dislike having your dignity ruffled, if you feel you've been overlooked or not been shown the respect you feel you're due, you may become huffy and haughty. But if real trouble strikes, your sterling qualities surface. With infinite courage, you will rally your forces and almost always come up trumps.

Sun in Taurus with Moon in Virgo

Oliver Cromwell	Maureen Lipman	Shirley MacLaine
Jack Nicholson	Laurence Olivier	Donatella Versace

As you take pride in doing things well, producing finely crafted work gives you a quiet sense of happiness and satisfaction and you can be a gifted problem-solver. Finding workable, practical solutions is your speciality. In business, you are well-suited to administrative or executive positions. In creative fields, you make a skilled artist and craftsperson, going to endless trouble to get the finished article just right. Oliver Cromwell famously demanded that his portrait should be painted properly, 'warts and all'. You have fastidious high standards and can be fiercely self-critical of yourself, and others whom you believe have botched up a job. Be careful not to get into know-it-all mode here! While you'll enjoy ticking off achievements on those never-ending to-do lists that whirr round in your head, it's not wise to let them run your life. Being rushed or surprised can get you flustered. It's often best to have one task on your desk at a time and give yourself time to finish one properly before you start on another.

As you are naturally responsible and conservative, unless Aries, Leo or Sagittarius is strong in your chart, spontaneity doesn't feature large. All that work and little play could make life a little dull. Some creative chaos could be just what you need. Hanging about with wild friends and letting your hair down occasionally could do you the world of good. A familiar domestic schedule is a major source of comfort but when you feel insecure you'll tend to work harder and go into obsessive little rituals, often around body care or exercise. Simplicity suits you well so cutting down to essentials and de-junking your life could be a perfect tonic from time to time.

Taurus Sun with Moon in Libra

Judy Collins	Zara Phillips	Sergei Prokofiev
Bertrand Russell	Rudolph Valentino	Richard Wilhelm

Peace and justice are vitally important for your sense of security, but you may sometimes be tempted to settle for peace at any price, as you also like to be liked. Not so for philosopher Bertrand Russell, who in old age campaigned vigorously for nuclear disarmament. It is often difficult for you to grasp the fact that some people are just not as idealistic, or as principled, as you are, and it can take a few hard knocks to shake you out of your ivory tower. Your tendency to see everyone else's point of view, as well as a distaste for confrontation, can prevent you from sticking up for yourself even when it's appropriate. But anyone who thinks you are a pushover is in for a big surprise if they go too far. Then the scales will swing back and whack them soundly off-balance. For such a charmer, you pack a hefty punch. Every last injustice will erupt out of you in a stream of passionate invective, leaving you drained and shaken. For you, balance matters, and if things get too nice, you'll stir up some trouble and strife to compensate.

You are an excellent strategic planner and have a knack of getting people on your side through tact and diplomacy. They can even end up doing exactly what you want, all the while thinking it was their idea in the first place – which suits you well, as you like to be in control. Without a partner, business or romantic, you are at a bit of a loss and in love you are sensual and gracious. Silent movie star Rudolph Valentino was, in his day, the epitome of romance. A home full of artwork, flowers and light feeds your soul and an escape to the country when things get tense and rough can keep you sane.

Taurus Sun with Moon in Scorpio

| Herbert Spencer | Paula Yates | Harry S Truman |
| Margaret Rutherford | Anthony Trollope | Koo Stark |

As you are wary of what might happen if your dark and intense feelings escaped and let rip, you tend to keep them well zippered up. Around you is an aura of barely suppressed passion, sexuality and power which is magnetically charismatic but threatening to those that would cross you. You make a rock-solid friend but a fearsome enemy. As children, many with this combination have encountered bullying, betrayal or suppressed information, leaving them feeling that the world is unsafe and no one can be trusted. Paula Yates only found out as an adult that her biological father was TV celebrity Hughie Green. Life is a serious matter for you, and you can be secretive, sometimes to the point of paranoia, not allowing anyone to get too close, believing that survival depends on constant vigilance. The philosopher Herbert Spencer suggested that societies evolve naturally by competing for resources and coined the phrase 'the survival of the fittest'. If you've been hurt, you could turn cynical, pessimistic or self-destructive, with a tendency to feed off bad news and tragedy. Your greatest challenge is to refuse to be a victim and use your formidable willpower, insight and honesty to drop the past and create a better future for everyone, including yourself.

If you can justify it to yourself, you are capable of extreme solutions to gain control. US President Harry S Truman did this after the Second World War, sanctioning dropping the atom bomb on Japan to ensure world peace. His phrase 'If you can't stand the heat get out of the kitchen' is one that is dear to your heart. You may need to deal with a tendency to be jealous and rather domineering but when you've learned to trust you can be kind, tender, affectionate and fiercely loyal.

Taurus Sun with Moon in Sagittarius

Margot Fonteyn	John Hannah	Glenda Jackson
Jiddu Krishnamurti	Liberace	Al Pacino

You hate restrictions and limitations and much prefer to make up your own rules as you go along. Your Moon wants to take risks, to open up to fresh ideas and experiences and explore the world and all that is in it, but your Sun demands stability, certainty and financial security. It all depends which one of them dominates. Your challenge is to find some way of having them both in equal measure. Sunny Sagittarius gives you faith in life and trust in the future, as well as a compelling wanderlust that can be physical, mental or restlessly romantic. You'd love to follow your dreams wherever they lead. To find the meaning of life is your crock of gold at the end of the rainbow, for you're almost certainly a natural philosopher and may be spiritually inclined. When you've found a fresh nugget of wisdom, you love to pass it on. You make an excellent teacher and a warm and inspiring guide to those under your care. Giving advice – and having it heeded – gives you a warm glow of satisfaction. You may have scholarly tastes or long to travel or to come into contact with foreign cultures. With your passionate delivery, you can inspire your listeners for good or ill.

You adore comfort and luxury and like to be noticed. Some with this combination like to make a splash and have a flair for drama and theatrical extravagance, like Liberace, with his sequinned suits and piano-shaped swimming pool. It's often the case that a Sagittarius Moon and its money are soon partying, yet creating something substantial and enduring is also a perpetual quest. Happily, you could be a shrewd entrepreneur, trusting your hunches to bring home the bacon.

Taurus Sun with Moon in Capricorn

Mark David Chapman	Yehudi Menuhin	Issey Miyake
Cher	Tammy Wynette	Adolf Hitler

With your admirable self-discipline and ability to plan long-term, you're a hard act to beat. Once you've set your sights on a goal, you will stick at it doggedly, overcoming every obstacle until success is yours. The problem is that you have a stern inner judge that can make your life miserable if you let it have its way. Many people with this combination have had childhoods where they had to grow up too soon, either from loss or deprivation or through having to conform dutifully to other people's specifications. It can be hard for you to believe that it is OK for you to be just the way you are without having to work hard to deserve praise, acceptance and warm affection, all of the things you crave so much. You're prone to hiding emotional needs for fear of disapproval and being quite judgmental and punishing of those you call whiners and victims. The dangers of this can be seen from the seriously repressed example of Adolf Hitler.

The positive side of this is that you are more than capable of looking after yourself and can be highly responsible about practically everything you do. You've an earthy sense of humour and an ironic take on life that often covers up a deep layer of sadness. Curiously enough, periods of solitude and basking in melancholy are often just what's needed to pick you up. Prestige and public recognition matter a great deal and this, combined with your fear of poverty and loss of control, can sometimes lead to obsessive workaholism and a streak of miserliness. Your challenge is to revel in life in the here and now, enjoying the sunshine and the sweet smell of well-earned success.

Taurus Sun with Moon in Aquarius

Tony Blair	Charlotte Brontë	George Lucas
Niccolo Machiavelli	Uma Thurman	Orson Welles

It is sometimes difficult for you to know what you're feeling as, instinctively, you respond more readily to the needs of society at large rather than to your own. Peace and social justice lie close to your heart and you can be more at ease with global issues than domestic concerns. If anybody tries to get too close, you may feel choked, making you seem aloof to others and possibly even a bit of an oddball or loner. You like things logical and clear-cut, yet your moods can be quite contrary. One moment you'll be chatty and friendly, then abrupt and withdrawn the next. Although you are highly ethical, you may sometimes believe, like

Machiavelli, advisor to medieval politicians, that the end justifies the means, completely missing the contradiction in that. You make a wonderful team player but, despite your need to challenge the established order, you like to be in control and are not always keen on having your own stance questioned.

Your home is likely to be unusual or unconventional in some way, but you may find it hard to put down roots, emotional or geographical, anywhere. For contentment, you need to find some way of opening and widening your family circle to let in the world. Quite often you are much more at home living in some kind of a community where you play a leading role. As your childhood may have been disrupted in some way or your mother detached, absent or independent – or perhaps eccentric or ahead of her time – no matter how long you have been in your home, you may have a sense of just camping, waiting for the call to move on.

Taurus Sun with Moon in Pisces

Ben Elton	Audrey Hepburn	Che Guevara
John Muir	Leonardo da Vinci	Debra Winger

You've the gift of being able to tap in to other people's desires, fantasies and feelings and appear to supply or express them, which is useful if you work with the public, especially in the media, arts, advertising – or the social services. Audrey Hepburn was voted, by *Vogue* magazine readers, the most stylish woman of all time. Understanding and trusting your intuition at work can lead to financial success. Being so sensitive and suggestible, you need to choose carefully whom you have around you. It's all too easy for you to be sucked into other people's realities and be pushed around or manipulated by stronger personalities — or possibly to do the same yourself. Poetry, nature and beauty are food for your soul but you may overlook order when it comes to domestic matters. A Pisces Moon, more often than not, means mess at home literally or metaphorically, but it's often best to see this as creative chaos, useful for stimulating your imagination for higher things.

Helping others will give you enormous satisfaction but you may need to guard against becoming a complete pushover for hard-luck stories. As you are so easily bruised yourself, and can identify with the victim, you hate to see people or animals suffer. Men with this combination can feel threatened by their tender feelings and suppress them firmly. You are good at fighting for the less fortunate but standing up for yourself isn't always easy. As a result, you can prefer to be reclusive or else to put on a tough, cynical front as a cover-up. Your task, as a sensual dreamer, is to bring the compassion, peace and beauty of heaven to earth in some practical way. A good example is John Muir, considered to be the father of the modern environmentalist movement, who started American National Parks to conserve and protect wildlife.

EIGHT

Mercury — It's All in the Mind

☿ THE GLYPHS FOR THE PLANETS ARE MADE UP OF THREE SYMBOLS: the circle, the semi-circle and the cross. Mercury is the only planet, apart from Pluto, whose glyph is made up of all three of these symbols. At the bottom there is the cross, representing the material world; at the top is the semi-circle of the crescent Moon, symbolising the personal soul; and in the middle, linking these two, is the circle of eternity, expressed through the individual. In mythology, Mercury was the only god who had access to all three worlds – the underworld, the middle world of earth and the higher world of the gods. Mercury in your chart represents your ability, through your thoughts and words, to make connections between the inner world of your mind and emotions, the outer world of other people and events, and the higher world of intuition. Your Mercury sign can give you a great deal of information about the way your mind works and about your interests, communication skills and your preferred learning style.

It can be frustrating when we just can't get through to some people and it's easy to dismiss them as being either completely thick or deliberately obstructive. Chances are they are neither. It may be that you're simply not talking each other's languages. Knowing your own and other people's communication styles can lead to major breakthroughs in relationships.

Information about children's natural learning patterns can help us teach them more effectively. It's impossible to learn properly if the material isn't presented in a way that resonates with the way your mind works. You just can't 'hear' it, pick it up or grasp it. Wires then get crossed and the data simply isn't processed. Many children are seriously disadvantaged if learning materials and environments don't speak to them. You may even have been a child like that yourself. If so, you could easily have been left with the false impression that you are a poor learner just because you couldn't get a handle on the lessons being taught. Identifying your own learning style can be like finding the hidden key to the treasure room of knowledge.

The signs of the zodiac are divided into four groups by element:

> The fire signs: Aries, Leo and Sagittarius
> The earth signs: Taurus, Virgo and Capricorn
> The air signs: Gemini, Libra and Aquarius
> The water signs: Cancer, Scorpio and Pisces

Your Mercury will therefore belong to one of the four elements, depending on which sign it is in. Your Mercury can only be in one of three signs – the same sign as your Sun, the one before or the one after. This means that each sign has one learning style that is never natural to it. For Taurus, this is the water style.

Mercury in each of the elements has a distinctive way of

operating. I've given the following names to the learning and communicating styles of Mercury through the elements. Mercury in fire – active imaginative; Mercury in earth – practical; Mercury in air – logical; and Mercury in water – impressionable.

Mercury in Fire: Active Imaginative

Your mind is wide open to the excitement of fresh ideas. It responds to action and to the creative possibilities of new situations. Drama, games and storytelling are excellent ways for you to learn. You love to have fun and play with ideas. Any material to be learned has to have some significance for you personally, or add to your self-esteem, otherwise you rapidly lose interest. You learn by acting out the new information, either physically or in your imagination. The most efficient way of succeeding in any goal is to make first a mental picture of your having achieved it. This is called mental rehearsal and is used by many top sportsmen and women as a technique to help improve their performance. You do this spontaneously, as your imagination is your greatest mental asset. You can run through future scenarios in your mind's eye and see, instantly, where a particular piece of information or situation could lead and spot possibilities that other people couldn't even begin to dream of. You are brilliant at coming up with flashes of inspiration for creative breakthroughs and crisis management.

Mercury in Earth: Practical

Endless presentations of feelings, theories and possibilities can make your eyes glaze over and your brain ache to shut down. What really turns you on is trying out these theories and possibilities to see if they work in practice. If they don't, you'll tend to classify them 'of no further interest'. Emotionally charged information is at best a puzzling non-starter and at worst an irritating turn-off. Practical demonstrations, tried and tested facts and working models fascinate you. Hands-on learning, where you can see how a process functions from start to finish, especially if it leads to some useful material end-product, is right up your street. It's important to allow yourself plenty of time when you are learning, writing or thinking out what to say, otherwise you can feel rushed and out of control, never pleasant sensations for earth signs. Your special skill is in coming up with effective solutions to practical problems and in formulating long-range plans that bring concrete, measurable results.

Mercury in Air: Logical

You love learning about, and playing with, ideas, theories and principles. Often you do this best by arguing or bouncing ideas off other people, or by writing down your thoughts. Your special gift is in your ability to stand back and work out the patterns of relationship between people or things. You much prefer it when facts are presented to you logically and unemotionally and have very little time for the irrational, uncertainty or for personal opinions. You do, though, tend to have plenty of those kinds of views yourself, only you call them logical conclusions. Whether a fact is useful or not is less important than whether it fits into your mental map of how the world operates. If facts don't fit in, you'll either ignore them, find a way of making them fit, or, occasionally, make a grand leap to a new, upgraded theory. Yours is the mind of the scientist or chess player. You make a brilliant planner because you can be detached enough to take an overview of the entire situation.

Mercury in Water: Impressionable

Your mind is sensitive to atmospheres and emotional undertones and to the context in which information is presented. Plain facts and figures can often leave you cold and even intimidated. You can take things too personally and read between the lines for what you believe is really being said or taught. If you don't feel emotionally safe, you can be cautious about revealing your true thoughts. It may be hard, or even impossible, for you to learn properly in what you sense is a hostile environment. You are excellent at impression management. Like a skilful artist painting a picture, you can influence others to think what you'd like them to by using suggestive gestures or pauses and intonations. People with Mercury in water signs are often seriously disadvantaged by left-brain schooling methods that are too rigidly structured for them. You take in information best through pictures or images, so that you get a 'feel' for the material and can make an emotional bond with it, in the same way you connect with people. In emotionally supportive situations where there is a rapport between you and your instructors, or your learning material, you are able just to drink in and absorb circulating knowledge without conscious effort, sometimes not even being clear about how or why you know certain things.

Finding Your Mercury Sign

If you don't yet know your Mercury sign, you might like to see if you can guess what it is from the descriptions below before checking it out in the tables on pp. 113–15.

Taurus Sun with Mercury in Aries

Tony Blair	David Attenborough	Adolf Hitler
Charlotte Brontë	Joanna Lumley	Al Pacino

Taureans have the reputation of being slow to anger. In general, that's true but with Mercury in Aries expect some sparks to fly. Your mind works best when stimulated with fresh, and preferably challenging, ideas and information. Controversy and combat attract your attention and you can more than hold your own in an argument. In fact, you're gifted at goading others into starting them. Your brain lights up where there is excitement and action, preferably some in which you can become directly involved. You warm to ideas which are the mental equivalent of throwing down the gauntlet, but sometimes you'll respond more like a bull to a red rag if you are crossed. It has been argued that it was Hitler's anger at the way Germany was treated after the First World War that led to the devastation of the Second World War.

When bored you'll just switch off and wander off into your private dream world. If what is being discussed or taught fires your imagination, you can grasp facts and sum up situations in double-quick time and can have uncannily accurate flashes of intuition about their possibilities. By working things through at lightning speed in your imagination, your mind moves seamlessly from input stimulus to action plan. As part of a team, you are a brilliant brainstormer and have the mental courage to put forward pioneering, daring and sometimes aggressive suggestions that would have more conservative Taureans – or anyone else for that matter – saying 'Hold on a minute . . .'.

In the heat of the moment you can come out with some

pretty cutting and sarcastic remarks that can wound deeply and are often best left unsaid. Snap first and check the data later, if at all, can be one of your less constructive traits. You are a rousing speaker, inspiring listeners to action and to follow whatever causes you are currently championing, so choosing your causes carefully is vitally important.

Taurus Sun with Mercury in Taurus

| David Beckham | Cher | Sigmund Freud |
| Yehudi Menuhin | Barbra Streisand | Rudolph Valentino |

There is often a deep sense of stillness about you that can sometimes be mistaken for passivity or even a lack of mental brilliance. While it is true that it can take you a long time to mull over and assimilate fresh ideas and information, you are unlikely to be dim. You need to savour anything new for a while until you have got its measure – to look at the facts, to touch base, to get the flavour of the situation, to tune in to the sense of it before you can take in fresh data and truly make it your own. Pushing you too quickly can make you pull up your mental drawbridge and refuse to even consider what you think is being forced on you.

Your attention is drawn to anything that gives you sensual pleasure and which you believe will lead towards your own peace and stability – and control of the situation. You have an eye for beauty and an ear for music and a mind focused on your bank balance or possessions, material or intellectual.

You have an immense loyalty to those ideas that you have so painstakingly made your own. Once you have made up your mind, it tends to stay that way, firm against any opposition. This can be an immense advantage in giving you the persistence to follow through on projects and to achieve substantial results. However, if it gets to the point where you reject out of hand any ideas other than your own, you can become inflexible and sometimes stubborn and downright closed-minded. Freud and Jung, the two giants of twentieth-century psychology, fell out when Freud refused to acknowledge the validity of Jung's ideas.

Taurus Sun with Mercury in Gemini

Judy Finnigan	Joseph Heller	Glenda Jackson
Niccolo Machiavelli	Richard Madeley	David O. Selznick

This is the least common Mercury sign to have with a Taurus Sun. With a Gemini Mercury, you are clever with words and love the mental thrill of making witty connections between odd ideas. Joseph Heller's bestselling black comedy *Catch 22* gives an example of Mercury in Gemini's quirky thinking. It is based on the idea that a fighter pilot who wants to be excused duty need only ask, but by asking he proves that he is sane, and is therefore fit to fly. Machiavelli, on the other hand, is an example of the combination of shrewd and practical Taurean common sense and Mercury in Gemini's capacity for spin. In his masterpiece *The Prince*, he advised rulers: 'If sometimes you need to conceal a fact with words do so in a way that it does not become known, or, if it does become known, that you have a ready and quick defence.' This was written in 1522. Some things never change.

You are less likely than the average Taurean to be a strong, silent type, as you are curious about almost everything and you thrive on frequent exchanges and communications. David O. Selznick, the American film mogul who produced *King Kong* and *Gone with the Wind*, liked to be involved in – and in control of – every single aspect of his productions and used to send barrages of notes to all his employees.

You are quick to notice new trends, often before everyone else, and love to pass on the information. Your head is likely to be well-stocked with curious facts and odd, seemingly useless, pieces of information, which you can produce at just the right moment, like a magician pulling a rabbit out of a hat. As you can quickly get bored, getting out and about and making new contacts keeps your wits sharp and lively.

NINE

Venus — At Your Pleasure

♀ THE GLYPH FOR VENUS IS MADE UP OF THE CIRCLE OF ETERNITY on top of the cross of matter. Esoterically this represents love, which is a quality of the divine, revealed on earth through personal choice. The saying 'One man's meat is another man's poison' couldn't be more relevant when it comes to what we love. It is a mystery why we find one thing attractive and another unattractive, or even repulsive. Looking at the sign, aspects and house of your Venus can't give any explanation of this mystery, but it can give some clear indications of what it is that you value and find desirable. This can be quite different from what current fashion tells you you should like. For example, many people are strongly turned on by voluptuous bodies but the media constantly shows images of near-anorexics as the desirable ideal. If you ignore what you, personally, find beautiful and try to be, or to love, what at heart leaves you cold, you are setting yourself up for unnecessary pain and dissatisfaction. Being true to your Venus sign, even if other people think you are strange, brings joy and pleasure. It also builds up your self-esteem because it grounds you solidly in your own personal values. This, in turn, makes you much more attractive to others. Not only that, it improves your relationships immeasurably, because you are living authentically and not betraying yourself by trying to prove your worth to others by being something you are not.

Glittering Venus, the brightest planet in the heavens, was named after the goddess of love, war and victory. Earlier names for her were Aphrodite, Innana and Ishtar. She was beautiful, self-willed and self-indulgent but was also skilled in all the arts of civilisation.

Your Venus sign shows what you desire and would like to possess, not only in relationships but also in all aspects of your taste, from clothes and culture to hobbies and hobby-horses. It identifies how and where you can be charming and seductive and skilful at creating your own type of beauty yourself. It also describes your style of attracting partners and the kind of people that turn you on. When your Venus is activated you feel powerful, desirable and wonderfully, wickedly indulged and indulgent. When it is not, even if someone has all the right credentials to make a good match, the relationship will always lack that certain something. If you don't take the chance to express your Venus to a good enough degree somewhere in your life, you miss out woefully on delight and happiness.

Morning Star, Evening Star

Venus appears in the sky either in the morning or in the evening. The ancients launched their attacks when Venus became a morning star, believing that she was then in her warrior-goddess role, releasing aggressive energy for victory in battle. If you're a morning-star person, you're likely to be impulsive, self-willed and idealistic, prepared to hold out until you find the partner who is just right for you.

Relationships and business dealings of morning-star Venus people are said to prosper best whenever Venus in the sky is a morning star. If you are an early bird, you can check this out. At these times Venus can be seen in the eastern sky before the Sun has risen.

The name for Venus as an evening star is Hesperus and it was then, traditionally, said to be sacred to lovers. Evening-star people tend to be easy-going and are open to negotiation, conciliation and making peace. If you are an evening-star Venus person, your best times in relationship and business affairs are said to be when Venus can be seen, jewel-like, in the western sky after the Sun has set.

Because the orbit of Venus is so close to the Sun, your Venus can only be in one of five signs. You have a morning-star Venus if your Venus is in one of the two signs that come before your Sun sign in the zodiac. You have an evening-star Venus if your Venus is in either of the two signs that follow your Sun sign. If you have Venus in the same sign as your Sun, you could be either, depending on whether your Venus is ahead of or behind your Sun. (You can find out which at the author's website www.janeridderpatrick.com.)

If you don't yet know your Venus sign, you might like to read through all of the following descriptions and see if you can guess what it is. You can find out for sure on pp. 116–18

At the beginning of each section are the names of some well-known Taureans with that particular Venus sign. You can find out more about them in Chapter Ten, Famous Taurus Birthdays.

Sun in Taurus with Venus in Aries

Tony Blair	Charlotte Brontë	Sir Fitzroy MacLean
Katharine Hepburn	Ian Rankin	Jeremy Paxman

You tend to be attracted to strong-minded types whom you may try to dominate but are never quite able to – and that is the way you like it. Any partner who would submit to your control would never earn or keep your respect. There may also be a competitiveness, healthy or otherwise, between you and your lovers, or rivals, for first place. Many men with this combination are attracted to women who are powerful and successful in their own right. Tony Blair's wife, Cherie, is a highly respected lawyer at the top of her own field, and earns far more than her Prime Minister husband does. Women with this mix tend to be headstrong and independent in their choice of partner. You are well able to stand up for yourself and have no hesitation about doing so if need be. In fact, there is nothing like a bit of conflict to keep your juices flowing.

Action, risk and danger – physical, mental or romantic – turn you on and you may find yourself drawn to situations where you put yourself on the line, whether this is skydiving, brinkmanship or flirting with life-and-death situations. In fact, a bit like James Bond, who was modelled on the Scottish diplomat and soldier, Sir Fitzroy MacLean. You can get carried away by the excitement of the moment. Venus in Aries is direct and to the point. When you want something – or someone – you want that urgently and you want it *now*. It pays to wait till the flames of passion die down (sometimes sooner than expected) before making a commitment. Once you are fully committed, however, you tend to stay loyal, true and touchingly romantic.

Sun in Taurus with Venus in Taurus

| Glenda Jackson | Karl Marx | Jessica Lange |
| Alan Titchmarsh | Issey Miyake | Leonardo da Vinci |

This placement of Venus heightens the Taurean love of beauty and of the earth and nature, as well as the finer things in life – good food and drink and sex. You have an artist's responsiveness to colour and quality and tend to choose partners who are both easy on the eye and financially solvent. Money is important for you and even on a tight budget you'll probably manage to give the impression of wealth. Some of you may not even be averse to marrying for money since you find it so much easier to be open and affectionate in affluent surroundings. Once committed, you're unlikely to stray unless quality sex or stability disappear from the menu. Since we often envy those who have what we want, but lack, it is tempting to speculate whether Karl Marx's passionate fist-shaking at the moneyed classes was not a little linked with his own desire for plenty.

You blossom when you have wealth and security enough to live in peace and comfort. Being sensual, rather than blatantly sexy, your very presence can be reassuring and comforting. You need to be wary of trying to control your partner or position if you feel insecure. Jealousy and looking on your partner as a possession rather than a person can undermine even the best of relationships. You tend to be old-fashioned, romantically inclined and love to be quietly spoiled in your turn, but your preference for a solid, reliable partner, who you know will always be there for you, means that you may choose to stay in a relationship long after its expiry date has come and gone.

Sun in Taurus with Venus in Gemini

David Beckham	Cher	Ben Elton
Maureen Lipman	Clement Freud	Yehudi Menuhin

It's easy for you to get on with practically anybody but a relationship where there is no rapport on the mental level will rarely get past first base with you. If the vital six inches between your ears aren't stimulated, you can quickly become bored. You are drawn to lively people who have plenty to say and who can feed your appetite for fresh and interesting topics of conversation. If they can make you laugh, so much the better. As you love to play with words yourself, and are quick to spot the ridiculous and incongruous in any situation, you like a partner who will share your appreciation of the quirkier side of life. It is often a good idea if you can take frequent breaks from each other so that when you do come back together again there is always something new and interesting to report. Once committed, you are well able to be faithful as long as your mind is fed and you have plenty of freedom of movement. When uncommitted, you may prefer to indulge your curiosity, sipping and sampling a variety of relationships. Many with this combination are hesitant about committing, preferring to keep their options open for as long as possible or have partners who don't like being tied down themselves.

Communication is the name of the game for you and you need a lot of response from your partner. You've a wonderful way with words and can be an accomplished flirt and flatterer and highly skilled at aural sex – or if you are not, your partner is likely to be. Friendship and comradeship are essential to you. Many comedians, both amateur and professional, for example Maureen Lipman and Joanna Lumley, have this line-up, combining Gemini wit and Taurean love of pranks.

Sun in Taurus with Venus in Cancer

| J.M. Barrie | Robert Browning | Margot Fonteyn |
| Liberace | Florence Nightingale | James Stewart |

You are lovingly attentive to the needs and emotional well-being of others. Nurturing, caring and protecting, especially towards those who are vulnerable, and allowing them to flourish by cherishing the best in them, can bring you great joy. Male or female, you tend to mother your partners or want them to mother you. Like J.M. Barrie's character Peter Pan, some with this combination would prefer never to grow up; being taken care of is just so delightful. Quiet companionship at home, and nights in with those you love, cocooned together away from the world outside, keeps you content. Margot Fonteyn, the leading ballerina of her day, chose to spend her retirement on a plantation in the seclusion of the Panamanian jungle, well away from the public eye, nursing her husband who had been paralysed by an assassin's bullet.

As you are deeply romantic, you long for gestures of love and affection. Being held, stroked and cuddled turns you on, but you may have to work through some shyness before you'll accept this freely. Be careful that you don't make a habit of putting other people's needs before your own, as you'll start to build up resentment if you are not receiving your fair share in return. Because you are fiercely loyal, dependable and devoted to those you care for, you're likely to attract the same back unless you make the mistake of trying to bind loved ones to you by subtle ties of obligation. This fear of loss can sometimes make it difficult for you to be emotionally honest until you feel totally secure; and being so sensitive to slights, you can be terrified of being humiliated, rejected or abandoned. It's essential to check the facts if you're feeling vulnerable, for your imagination then tends to operate in overdrive. Facts, you'll find, are friendly.

Sun in Taurus with Venus in Pisces

Queen Elizabeth II	Shirley MacLaine	Barbra Streisand
Tammy Wynette	Michelle Pfeiffer	John Mortimer

You yearn for emotional intimacy and the complete fusion of two souls, but you may find this hard to express, or even find words to describe, because of the Taurean discomfort with open displays of emotion. You are capable of devoted, sometimes self-sacrificial, love and there can be an idealistic quality to your affections. At its highest level, you'll find deep satisfaction in spiritual surrender and serving others unselfishly. If you are more sensually inclined, the combination of earthy Taurus and glamorous Venus in Pisces sometimes leads to a tendency to fall in love, or be seduced, at the drop of a hat – but what you think you see is often not what you get. You are acutely attuned to your lover's fantasies and can lose yourself in trying to become his or her ideal partner.

You're often drawn to people who are vulnerable or emotionally unavailable or who need rescuing or fixing in some way. They may then become dependent and not always be as attentive to your needs as you'd like. It's very hard for you to say no to those you love, even if this causes you suffering. There is something about the anguish of unrequited love that pulls you like a magnet and once a relationship is established, you find it hard to let go, so be careful not to lose sight of your own desires in the process and to put them at the back of the queue for attention. Music can be a profoundly meaningful way of helping you express and release your emotional pleasure and pain. Tammy Wynette's soulful 'Stand by Your Man' just about sums up your attitude to relationships.

TEN

Famous Taurus Birthdays

FIND OUT WHO SHARES YOUR MOON, MERCURY AND VENUS SIGNS, and any challenging Sun aspects, and see what they have done with the material they were born with. Notice how often it is not just the personalities of the people themselves but the roles of actors, characters of authors and works of artists that reflect their astrological make-up. In reading standard biographies, I've been constantly astounded – and, of course, delighted – at how often phrases used to describe individuals could have been lifted straight from their astrological profiles. Check it out yourself!

A few people below have been given a choice of two Moons. This is because the Moon changed sign on the day that they were born and no birth time was available. You may be able to guess which one is correct if you read the descriptions of the Moon signs in Chapter Seven.

20 April
1889 Adolf Hitler, German dictator, responsible for 30 million deaths
Sun aspects: none
Moon: Capricorn   Mercury: Aries   Venus: Taurus

21 April
1926 Elizabeth II, Queen of the United Kingdom and Head of the Commonwealth
Sun aspects: none
Moon: Leo   Mercury: Aries   Venus: Pisces

22 April
1937 Jack Nicholson, actor, *One Flew over the Cuckoo's Nest*
Sun aspects: Uranus, Pluto
Moon: Virgo   Mercury: Taurus   Venus: Aries

23 April
1775 Joseph Turner, English watercolour and landscape artist
Sun aspects: Pluto
Moon: Aquarius   Mercury: Aries   Venus: Taurus

24 April
1942 Barbra Streisand, American singer and actress, *Funny Girl*
Sun aspects: Pluto
Moon: Leo   Mercury: Taurus   Venus: Pisces

25 April
1940 Al Pacino, actor, *The Godfather*
Sun aspects: Saturn, Pluto
Moon: Sagittarius   Mercury: Aries   Venus: Gemini

26 April
1916 Morris West, writer, *The Devil's Advocate*, *The Shoes of the Fisherman*
Sun aspects: Neptune
Moon: Aquarius   Mercury: Taurus   Venus: Gemini

27 April
1759 Mary Wollstonecraft, early feminist and author, *A Vindication of the Rights of Woman*
Sun aspects: Neptune
Moon: Taurus   Mercury: Taurus   Venus: Gemini

28 April
1974 Penélope Cruz, actress, *Captain Corelli's Mandolin*
Sun aspects: none
Moon: Cancer   Mercury: Taurus   Venus: Pisces

29 April
1863 William Randolph Hearst, American newspaper magnate
Sun aspects: Pluto
Moon: Virgo   Mercury: Taurus   Venus: Gemini

30 April
1945 Annie Dillard, mystic and writer, *Pilgrim at Tinker Creek*
Sun aspects: Pluto
Moon: Sagittarius   Mercury: Aries   Venus: Aries

1 May
1946 Joanna Lumley, actress and comedian, *Absolutely Fabulous*
Sun aspects: Pluto
Moon: Taurus   Mercury: Aries   Venus: Taurus

2 May
1975 David Beckham, captain of the English football team
Sun aspects: none
Moon: Capricorn/Aquarius   Mercury: Taurus   Venus: Gemini

3 May
1959 Ben Elton, comedian and scriptwriter, *Blackadder*, *The Thin Blue Line*
Sun aspects: Uranus, Neptune
Moon: Pisces   Mercury: Aries   Venus: Gemini

4 May
1929 Audrey Hepburn, elegant actress, *My Fair Lady*, *Breakfast at Tiffany's*
Sun aspects: none
Moon: Pisces   Mercury: Gemini   Venus: Aries

5 May
1818 Karl Marx, father of Communism, *Das Kapital*, *The Communist Manifesto*
Sun aspects: none
Moon: Taurus   Mercury: Gemini   Venus: Taurus

6 May
1856 Sigmund Freud, father of psychoanalysis
Sun aspects: Uranus
Moon: Gemini   Mercury: Taurus   Venus: Aries

7 May
1919 Eva Perón, actress and wife of Argentine president, inspiration for *Evita*
Sun aspects: Saturn, Neptune
Moon: Leo   Mercury: Aries   Venus: Gemini

8 May
1828 Jean Henri Dunant, instigator of the International Red Cross
Sun aspects: none
Moon: Pisces   Mercury: Taurus   Venus: Cancer

9 May
1873 Howard Carter, discoverer of the treasure-filled tomb of Tut'ankhamun
Sun aspects: Pluto
Moon: Libra   Mercury: Aries   Venus: Taurus

10 May
1873 Richard Wilhelm, translator of the Chinese oracle, *I Ching*
Sun aspects: Pluto
Moon: Libra   Mercury: Aries   Venus: Taurus

11 May
1904 Salvador Dalí, surrealist painter
Sun aspects: Saturn
Moon: Aries   Mercury: Taurus   Venus: Taurus

12 May

1820 Florence Nightingale, 'The Lady with the Lamp', founder of professional nursing
Sun aspects: none
Moon: Taurus   Mercury: Aries   Venus: Cancer

13 May

1950 Stevie Wonder, American musician, 'My Cherie Amour'
Sun aspects: Pluto
Moon: Aries   Mercury: Taurus   Venus: Aries

14 May

1944 George Lucas, film director, *American Graffiti*, *Star Wars*
Sun aspects: none
Moon: Aquarius   Mercury: Taurus   Venus: Taurus

15 May

1937 Madeleine Albright, first woman US Secretary of State.
Sun aspects:none
Moon: Cancer/Leo   Mercury: Taurus   Venus: Aries

16 May

1955 Debra Winger, actress, *Terms of Endearment*
Sun aspects: Saturn, Pluto
Moon: Pisces   Mercury: Gemini   Venus: Aries

17 May

1749 Dr Edward Jenner, discoverer of vaccination
Sun aspects: Uranus, Pluto
Moon: Gemini   Mercury: Taurus   Venus: Taurus

18 May
1919 Dame Margot Fonteyn, one of the finest ballerinas of all time
Sun aspects: Saturn, Uranus
Moon: Sagittarius   Mercury: Taurus   Venus: Cancer

19 May
1925 Malcolm X, American black nationalist leader and civil-rights activist
Sun aspects: Neptune
Moon: Aries   Mercury: Taurus   Venus: Gemini

20 May
1946 Cher, American singer and entertainer, 'I Got You Babe', 'Believe'
Sun aspects: none
Moon: Capricorn   Mercury: Taurus   Venus: Gemini

Other Taurus people mentioned in this book
Susan Atkins, member of the Manson 'family' who killed the pregnant Sharon Tate ☆ David Attenborough, broadcaster and producer of nature documentaries ☆ J.M. Barrie, author, *Peter Pan* ☆ Tony Blair, British prime minister ☆ Cate Blanchett, actress, *Elizabeth* ☆ Lucrezia Borgia, illegitimate daughter of Pope Alexander VI ☆ Charlotte Brontë, author, *Jane Eyre* ☆ Robert Browning, poet, *The Ring and the Book* ☆ Catherine the Great, Empress of Russia with many lovers ☆ David Mark Chapman, killer of John Lennon ☆ Judy Collins, singer, 'Both Sides Now' ☆ Bing Crosby, singer, 'White Chistmas' ☆ Sandra Dee, actress, *A Summer Place* ☆ Sir Walter de la Mare, poet, *The Listeners* ☆ Daphne Du Maurier, novelist, *Rebecca* ☆ Brian Eno, composer and producer of rock music ☆ Linda Evangelista, supermodel ☆ Gabriel Fauré, composer best known for his *Requiem* ☆ Judy

Finnigan, TV presenter ☆ Clement Freud, broadcaster and caterer, 'Just a Minute' ☆ Tony Hancock, radio personality, *Hancock's Half Hour* ☆ John Hannah, actor who played fellow Taurean Ian Rankin's character, Inspector Rebus ☆ Joseph Heller, author, *Catch 22* ☆ Katharine Hepburn, actress, *The African Queen* ☆ Glenda Jackson, actress and politician, *Women in Love* ☆ Sid James, comedian with dirty laugh, *Carry On Up the Khyber* ☆ Jim Jones, cult leader and murderer of 914 of his followers ☆ Jiddu Krishnamurti, spiritual teacher of the philosophy of self-reliance and awareness ☆ Jessica Lange, actress, *The Postman Always Rings Twice* ☆ Edward Lear, artist and humorist, *A Book of Nonsense* ☆ Liberace, flamboyant pianist ☆ Maureen Lipman, comedian, actress and columnist, 'Beattie' in the BT ads ☆ Shirley MacLaine, actress, dancer and esoteric writer, *Terms of Endearment* ☆ Sir Fitzroy MacLean, Scottish diplomat, soldier and writer, the model for James Bond ☆ Niccolo Machiavelli, Italian statesman and political philosopher, *The Prince* ☆ Richard Madeley, TV presenter ☆ Guglielmo Marconi, inventor of the wireless telegraph ☆ Yehudi Menuhin, violinist and founder of a school for musically gifted children ☆ Issey Miyake, fashion designer ☆ John Mortimer, dramatist, novelist and barrister, *Rumpole of the Bailey* ☆ Daniela Nardini, actress, *This Life* ☆ Laurence Olivier, actor, *Rebecca* ☆ Robert Owen, social reformer and builder of the model village of New Lanark ☆ Jeremy Paxman, irascible TV presenter ☆ Michelle Pfeiffer, actress, *Dangerous Liaisons* ☆ Zara Phillips, daughter of Princess Anne ☆ Sergei Prokofiev, composer, *Romeo and Juliet* ☆ Ian Rankin, crime writer, creator of Inspector Rebus ☆ Bertrand Russell, philosopher, mathematician and activist for nuclear disarmament ☆ Margaret Rutherford, actress, Agatha Christie's genteel detective, Miss Jane Marple ☆ Sheila Scott, model, actress and record-breaking aviator ☆ David O. Selznick, film producer, *Gone With the Wind* ☆ Herbert Spencer, English philosopher and advocate of 'social Darwinism', the survival of the fittest ☆ Benjamin Spock, paediatrician, *The Common Sense Book of Baby and Child Care* ☆ Koo Stark, actress and photographer once linked romantically with Prince Andrew ☆ James Stewart, actor, *It's a Wonderful Life* ☆ David Suchet, actor who played Agatha Christie's fusspot detective Hercule Poirot and starred in fellow Taurean Anthony Trollope's *The Way We Live Now* ☆ Shirley Temple, precocious child star, later American diplomat ☆ Denis Thatcher, successful businessman and husband of former prime minister Margaret Thatcher ☆ Uma Thurman, actress, *Dangerous Liaisons* ☆ Alan Titchmarsh, TV gardener ☆ Anthony Trollope, author *The Way We Live Now* ☆ Harry S Truman, US President who authorised dropping the first atom bombs on Japan ☆ Rudolph Valentino, silent screen legend, *The Sheik* ☆ Donatella Versace, Italian fashion entrepreneur ☆ Sid Vicious, punk musician with the Sex Pistols who murdered his girlfriend and died of a heroin overdose ☆ Orson Welles, film director, *Citizen Kane* ☆ Victoria Wood, actress and comedian, *Dinnerladies* ☆ Tammy Wynette, singer, 'Stand By Your Man' ☆ Paula Yates, TV presenter, *The Big Breakfast*, who died of a heroin overdose

ELEVEN

Finding Your Sun, Moon, Mercury and Venus Signs

ALL OF THE ASTROLOGICAL DATA IN THIS BOOK WAS CALCULATED by Astrolabe, who also supply a wide range of astrological software. I am most grateful for their help and generosity.

ASTROLABE, PO Box 1750, Brewster, MA 02631, USA
www.alabe.com

PLEASE NOTE THAT ALL OF THE TIMES GIVEN ARE IN GREENWICH MEAN TIME (GMT). If you were born during British Summer Time (BST) you will need to subtract one hour from your birth time to convert it to GMT. If you were born outside of the British Isles, find the time zone of your place of birth and the number of hours it is different from GMT. Add the difference in hours if you were born west of the UK, and subtract the difference if you were born east of the UK to convert your birth time to GMT.

Your Sun Sign

Check your year of birth, and if you were born between the dates and times given the Sun was in Taurus when you were born – confirming that you're a Taurean. If you were born before the time on the date that Taurus begins in your year, you are an Aries. If you were born after the time on the date Taurus ends in your year, you are a Gemini.

Your Moon Sign

The Moon changes sign every two and a half days. To find your Moon sign, first find your year of birth. You will notice that in each year box there are three columns.

The second column shows the day of the month that the Moon changed sign, while the first column gives the abbreviation for the sign that the Moon entered on that date.

In the middle column, the month has been omitted, so that the dates run from, for example, 20 to 30 (April) and then from 1 to 21 (May).

In the third column, after the star, the time that the Moon changed sign on that day is given.

Look down the middle column of your year box to find your date of birth. If your birth date is given, look to the third column to find the time that the Moon changed sign. If you were born after that time, your Moon sign is given in the first column next to your birth date. If you were born before that time, your Moon sign is the one above the one next to your birth date.

If your birth date is not given, find the closest date before it. The sign shown next to that date is your Moon sign.

If you were born on a day that the Moon changed signs and you do not know your time of birth, try out both of that day's Moon signs and feel which one fits you best.

The abbreviations for the signs are as follows:

Aries – Ari   Taurus – Tau   Gemini – Gem   Cancer – Can
Leo – Leo   Virgo – Vir   Libra – Lib   Scorpio – Sco
Sagittarius – Sag   Capricorn – Cap   Aquarius – Aqu   Pisces – Pis

Your Mercury Sign

Find your year of birth and then the column in which your birthday falls. Look up to the top of the column to find your Mercury sign. You will see that some dates appear twice. This is because Mercury changed sign that day. If your birthday falls on one of these dates, try out both Mercury signs and see which one fits you best. If you know your birth time, you can find out for sure which Mercury sign is yours on my website – www.janeridderpatrick.com.

Your Venus Sign

Find your year of birth and then the column in which your birthday falls. Look up to the top of the column to find your Venus sign. Some dates have two possible signs. That's because Venus changed signs that day. Try them both out and see which fits you best. If the year you are interested in doesn't appear in the tables, or you have Venus in the same sign as your Sun and want to know whether you have a morning or evening star Venus, you can find the information on my website – www.janeridderpatrick.com.

♉ Taurus Sun Tables ☉

YEAR	TAURUS BEGINS	TAURUS ENDS
1930	20 Apr 20.05	21 May 19.42
1931	21 Apr 01.39	22 May 01.15
1932	20 Apr 07.28	21 May 07.06
1933	20 Apr 13.18	21 May 12.56
1934	20 Apr 19.00	21 May 18.35
1935	21 Apr 00.50	22 May 00.24
1936	20 Apr 06.31	21 May 06.07
1937	20 Apr 12.19	21 May 11.57
1938	20 Apr 18.14	21 May 17.50
1939	20 Apr 23.55	21 May 23.26
1940	20 Apr 05.51	21 May 05.23
1941	20 Apr 11.50	21 May 11.22
1942	20 Apr 17.39	21 May 17.08
1943	20 Apr 23.31	21 May 23.02
1944	20 Apr 05.17	21 May 04.50
1945	20 Apr 11.06	21 May 10.40
1946	20 Apr 17.02	21 May 16.33
1947	20 Apr 22.39	21 May 22.09
1948	20 Apr 04.24	21 May 03.57
1949	20 Apr 10.17	21 May 09.50
1950	20 Apr 15.59	21 May 15.27
1951	20 Apr 21.48	21 May 21.15
1952	20 Apr 03.36	21 May 03.03
1953	20 Apr 09.25	21 May 08.52
1954	20 Apr 15.19	21 May 14.47
1955	20 Apr 20.57	21 May 20.24
1956	20 Apr 02.43	21 May 02.12
1957	20 Apr 08.41	21 May 08.10
1958	20 Apr 14.27	21 May 13.51
1959	20 Apr 20.16	21 May 19.42
1960	20 Apr 02.05	21 May 01.33
1961	20 Apr 07.55	21 May 07.22
1962	20 Apr 13.50	21 May 13.16
1963	20 Apr 19.36	21 May 18.58
1964	20 Apr 01.27	21 May 00.49
1965	20 Apr 07.26	21 May 06.50

YEAR	TAURUS BEGINS	TAURUS ENDS
1966	20 Apr 13.11	21 May 12.32
1967	20 Apr 18.55	21 May 18.17
1968	20 Apr 00.41	21 May 00.05
1969	20 Apr 06.26	21 May 05.49
1970	20 Apr 12.14	21 May 11.37
1971	20 Apr 17.54	21 May 17.15
1972	19 Apr 23.37	20 May 22.59
1973	20 Apr 05.30	21 May 04.53
1974	20 Apr 11.18	21 May 10.36
1975	20 Apr 10.07	21 May 16.23
1976	19 Apr 23.03	20 May 22.21
1977	20 Apr 04.57	21 May 04.14
1978	20 Apr 10.49	21 May 10.08
1979	20 Apr 16.35	21 May 15.53
1980	20 Apr 22.22	20 May 21.42
1981	20 Apr 04.18	21 May 03.39
1982	20 Apr 10.07	21 May 09.22
1983	20 Apr 15.50	21 May 15.06
1984	19 Apr 21.38	20 May 20.57
1985	20 Apr 03.25	21 May 02.42
1986	20 Apr 09.12	21 May 08.27
1987	20 Apr 14.57	21 May 14.10
1988	19 Apr 20.44	20 May 19.56
1989	20 Apr 02.39	21 May 01.53
1990	20 Apr 08.26	21 May 07.37
1991	20 Apr 14.08	21 May 13.20
1992	19 Apr 19.56	20 May 19.12
1993	20 Apr 01.49	21 May 01.01
1994	20 apr 07.36	21 May 06.48
1995	20 Apr 13.21	21 May 12.34
1996	19 Apr 19.09	20 May 18.23
1997	20 Apr 01.02	21 May 06.05
1998	20 Apr 06.56	21 May 06.05
1999	20 Apr 12.45	21 May 11.52
2000	19 Apr 18.39	20 May 17.49

♉ Taurus – Finding Your Moon Sign ☽

1930		
Aqu	20	*21:58
Pis	23	*10:22
Ari	25	*21:09
Tau	28	*05:07
Gem	30	*10:25
Can	2	*13:53
Leo	4	*16:31
Vir	6	*19:10
Lib	8	*22:30
Sco	11	*03:06
Sag	13	*09:39
Cap	15	*18:39
Aqu	18	*06:03
Pis	20	*18:33

1931		
Gem	20	*16:55
Can	23	*00:41
Leo	25	*06:03
Vir	27	*09:09
Lib	29	*10:34
Sco	1	*11:26
Sag	3	*13:14
Cap	5	*17:35
Aqu	8	*01:37
Pis	10	*13:02
Ari	13	*01:56
Tau	15	*13:53
Gem	17	*23:25
Can	20	*06:25

1932		
Sco	20	*20:33
Sag	22	*19:57
Cap	24	*21:15
Aqu	27	*02:05
Pis	29	*10:56
Ari	1	*22:46
Tau	4	*11:45
Gem	7	*00:19
Can	9	*11:33
Leo	11	*20:45
Vir	14	*03:12
Lib	16	*06:32
Sco	18	*07:14
Sag	20	*06:47

1933		
Pis	19	*15:54
Ari	22	*00:14
Tau	24	*10:31
Gem	26	*22:18
Can	29	*10:57
Leo	1	*23:05
Vir	4	*08:39
Lib	6	*14:15
Sco	8	*16:06
Sag	10	*15:42
Cap	12	*15:15
Aqu	14	*16:46
Pis	16	*21:34
Ari	19	*05:45

1934		
Can	19	*06:26
Leo	21	*19:09
Vir	24	*07:19
Lib	26	*16:31
Sco	28	*22:05
Sag	1	*01:01
Cap	3	*02:53
Aqu	5	*05:06
Pis	7	*08:26
Ari	9	*13:09
Tau	11	*19:23
Gem	14	*03:38
Can	16	*14:17
Leo	19	*02:54

ℝ Taurus – Finding Your Moon Sign ☽

1935		
Sco	19	*01:08
Sag	21	*09:05
Cap	23	*15:12
Aqu	25	*19:43
Pis	27	*22:39
Ari	30	*00:26
Tau	2	*02:09
Gem	4	*05:26
Can	6	*11:51
Leo	8	*21:55
Vir	11	*10:25
Lib	13	*22:47
Sco	16	*08:53
Sag	18	*16:12
Cap	20	*21:19

1936		
Ari	19	*11:19
Tau	21	*10:37
Gem	23	*10:38
Can	25	*13:23
Leo	27	*20:03
Vir	30	*06:22
Lib	2	*18:42
Sco	5	*07:16
Sag	7	*18:53
Cap	10	*04:56
Aqu	12	*12:46
Pis	14	*17:52
Ari	16	*20:13
Tau	18	*20:47
Gem	20	*21:12

1937		
Vir	20	*08:16
Lib	22	*17:50
Sco	25	*05:20
Sag	27	*18:04
Cap	30	*06:56
Aqu	2	*18:08
Pis	5	*01:55
Ari	7	*05:47
Tau	9	*06:31
Gem	11	*05:56
Can	13	*06:00
Leo	15	*08:27
Vir	17	*14:19
Lib	19	*23:35

1938		
Cap	20	*03:31
Aqu	22	*16:10
Pis	25	*02:52
Ari	27	*10:07
Tau	29	*14:00
Gem	1	*15:44
Can	3	*16:50
Leo	5	*18:41
Vir	7	*22:17
Lib	10	*04:05
Sco	12	*12:16
Sag	14	*22:41
Cap	17	*10:51
Aqu	19	*23:37

1939		
Tau	19	*18:56
Gem	22	*01:15
Can	24	*05:43
Leo	26	*08:54
Vir	28	*11:26
Lib	30	*14:02
Sco	2	*17:36
Sag	4	*23:11
Cap	7	*07:34
Aqu	9	*18:41
Pis	12	*07:09
Ari	14	*18:40
Tau	17	*03:27
Gem	19	*09:05

♉ Taurus – Finding Your Moon Sign ☽

1940		
Lib	20	*01:22
Sco	22	*01:33
Sag	24	*02:49
Cap	26	*06:49
Aqu	28	*14:39
Pis	1	*01:56
Ari	3	*14:51
Tau	6	*03:11
Gem	8	*13:32
Can	10	*21:32
Leo	13	*03:21
Vir	15	*07:17
Lib	17	*09:40
Sco	19	*11:11

1941		
Pis	21	*01:07
Ari	23	*12:34
Tau	26	*01:22
Gem	28	*14:10
Can	1	*01:55
Leo	3	*11:32
Vir	5	*18:05
Lib	7	*21:10
Sco	9	*21:33
Sag	11	*20:49
Cap	13	*21:04
Aqu	16	*00:16
Pis	18	*07:33
Ari	20	*18:34

1942		
Can	21	*00:09
Leo	23	*12:20
Vir	25	*22:01
Lib	28	*03:49
Sco	30	*05:59
Sag	2	*06:02
Cap	4	*06:04
Aqu	6	*07:56
Pis	8	*12:44
Ari	10	*20:31
Tau	13	*06:36
Gem	15	*18:14
Can	18	*06:49
Leo	20	*19:20

1943		
Sco	20	*12:02
Sag	22	*15:55
Cap	24	*18:39
Aqu	26	*21:21
Pis	29	*00:35
Ari	1	*04:39
Tau	3	*09:57
Gem	5	*17:15
Can	8	*03:17
Leo	10	*15:38
Vir	13	*04:21
Lib	15	*14:43
Sco	17	*21:18
Sag	20	*00:32

1944		
Ari	20	*15:35
Tau	22	*16:28
Gem	24	*18:58
Can	27	*00:49
Leo	29	*10:36
Vir	1	*23:04
Lib	4	*11:38
Sco	6	*22:17
Sag	9	*06:26
Cap	11	*12:32
Aqu	13	*17:09
Pis	15	*20:34
Ari	17	*23:03
Tau	20	*01:15

♉ Taurus – Finding Your Moon Sign ☽

1945		
Vir	21	*20:03
Lib	24	*08:14
Sco	26	*20:52
Sag	29	*08:55
Cap	1	*19:39
Aqu	4	*04:05
Pis	6	*09:19
Ari	8	*11:23
Tau	10	*11:24
Gem	12	*11:12
Can	14	*12:52
Leo	16	*17:56
Vir	19	*02:56

1946		
Cap	21	*20:27
Aqu	24	*07:55
Pis	26	*15:53
Ari	28	*19:44
Tau	30	*20:30
Gem	2	*20:03
Can	4	*20:23
Leo	6	*23:05
Vir	9	*04:57
Lib	11	*13:54
Sco	14	*01:08
Sag	16	*13:46
Cap	19	*02:41

1947		
Tau	21	*03:55
Gem	23	*06:27
Can	25	*08:22
Leo	27	*10:44
Vir	29	*14:15
Lib	1	*19:23
Sco	4	*02:35
Sag	6	*12:09
Cap	8	*23:55
Aqu	11	*12:40
Pis	14	*00:19
Ari	16	*08:55
Tau	18	*13:50
Gem	20	*15:50

1948		
Vir	19	*03:30
Lib	21	*05:16
Sco	23	*07:49
Sag	25	*12:32
Cap	27	*20:22
Aqu	30	*07:16
Pis	2	*19:43
Ari	5	*07:27
Tau	7	*16:47
Gem	9	*23:18
Can	12	*03:37
Leo	14	*06:38
Vir	16	*09:14
Lib	18	*12:07
Sco	20	*15:55

1949		
Aqu	20	*03:59
Pis	22	*15:08
Ari	25	*04:00
Tau	27	*16:40
Gem	30	*03:47
Can	2	*12:42
Leo	4	*19:10
Vir	6	*23:10
Lib	9	*01:06
Sco	11	*01:53
Sag	13	*02:57
Cap	15	*05:56
Aqu	17	*12:20
Pis	19	*22:26

♉ Taurus – Finding Your Moon Sign ☽

1950		
Gem	20	03:53
Can	22	16:01
Leo	25	01:56
Vir	27	08:28
Lib	29	11:23
Sco	1	11:36
Sag	3	10:50
Cap	5	11:09
Aqu	7	14:23
Pis	9	21:34
Ari	12	08:18
Tau	14	20:58
Gem	17	09:52
Can	19	21:50

1951		
Lib	19	*17:13
Sco	21	*19:54
Sag	23	*20:39
Cap	25	*21:20
Aqu	27	*23:33
Pis	30	*04:13
Ari	2	*11:26
Tau	4	*20:46
Gem	7	*07:50
Can	9	*20:12
Leo	12	*08:48
Vir	14	*19:43
Lib	17	*03:03
Sco	19	*06:22

1952		
Pis	19	*16:40
Ari	21	*19:56
Tau	24	*00:15
Gem	26	*06:40
Can	28	*16:06
Leo	1	*04:12
Vir	3	*16:57
Lib	6	*03:38
Sco	8	*10:47
Sag	10	*14:49
Cap	12	*17:08
Aqu	14	*19:14
Pis	16	*22:05
Ari	19	*02:07

1953		
Leo	20	*23:27
Vir	23	*11:52
Lib	26	*00:39
Sco	28	*11:51
Sag	30	*20:51
Cap	3	*03:54
Aqu	5	*09:11
Pis	7	*12:45
Ari	9	*14:48
Tau	11	*16:12
Gem	13	*18:26
Can	15	*23:17
Leo	18	*07:47
Vir	20	*19:30

1954		
Sag	20	*22:54
Cap	23	*10:10
Aqu	25	*19:01
Pis	28	*00:19
Ari	30	*02:07
Tau	2	*01:42
Gem	4	*01:07
Can	6	*02:31
Leo	8	*07:29
Vir	10	*16:22
Lib	13	*04:03
Sco	15	*16:41
Sag	18	*04:53
Cap	20	*15:48

♉ Taurus – Finding Your Moon Sign ☽

1955		
Ari	20	*09:28
Tau	22	*10:28
Gem	24	*10:24
Can	26	*11:09
Leo	28	*14:09
Vir	30	*19:58
Lib	3	*04:26
Sco	5	*15:04
Sag	8	*03:18
Cap	10	*16:18
Aqu	13	*04:28
Pis	15	*13:51
Ari	17	*19:20
Tau	19	*21:10

1956		
Vir	20	*06:16
Lib	22	*10:36
Sco	24	*16:44
Sag	27	*01:26
Cap	29	*12:44
Aqu	2	*01:27
Pis	4	*13:14
Ari	6	*22:04
Tau	9	*03:23
Gem	11	*06:00
Can	13	*07:20
Leo	15	*08:52
Vir	17	*11:40
Lib	19	*16:25

1957		
Cap	19	*09:08
Aqu	21	*19:53
Pis	24	*08:22
Ari	26	*20:21
Tau	29	*06:17
Gem	1	*13:45
Can	3	*19:07
Leo	5	*22:53
Vir	8	*01:36
Lib	10	*03:57
Sco	12	*06:48
Sag	14	*11:14
Cap	16	*18:13
Aqu	19	*04:12

1958		
Tau	19	*06:16
Gem	21	*18:02
Can	24	*03:45
Leo	26	*10:42
Vir	28	*14:39
Lib	30	*16:06
Sco	2	*16:14
Sag	4	*16:43
Cap	6	*19:21
Aqu	9	*01:30
Pis	11	*11:27
Ari	13	*23:57
Tau	16	*12:49
Gem	19	*00:12

1959		
Lib	21	*01:17
Sco	23	*01:33
Sag	25	*00:59
Cap	27	*01:33
Aqu	29	*04:55
Pis	1	*11:59
Ari	3	*22:19
Tau	6	*10:38
Gem	8	*23:34
Can	11	*11:56
Leo	13	*22:39
Vir	16	*06:37
Lib	18	*11:05
Sco	20	*12:23

♉ Taurus – Finding Your Moon Sign ☽

1960		
Pis	20	*19:55
Ari	23	*02:23
Tau	25	*10:51
Gem	27	*21:16
Can	30	*09:22
Leo	2	*21:58
Vir	5	*08:57
Lib	7	*16:29
Sco	9	*20:05
Sag	11	*20:54
Cap	13	*20:50
Aqu	15	*21:51
Pis	18	*01:24
Ari	20	*07:55

1961		
Can	20	*04:50
Leo	22	*16:43
Vir	25	*05:30
Lib	27	*16:33
Sco	30	*00:25
Sag	2	*05:24
Cap	4	*08:39
Aqu	6	*11:23
Pis	8	*14:22
Ari	10	*17:55
Tau	12	*22:25
Gem	15	*04:34
Can	17	*13:17
Leo	20	*00:45

1962		
Sco	20	*01:36
Sag	22	*11:26
Cap	24	*19:19
Aqu	27	*01:06
Pis	29	*04:39
Ari	1	*06:11
Tau	3	*06:49
Gem	5	*08:16
Can	7	*12:29
Leo	9	*20:36
Vir	12	*08:11
Lib	14	*21:02
Sco	17	*08:42
Sag	19	*18:02

1963		
Pis	19	*14:52
Ari	21	*16:29
Tau	23	*15:50
Gem	25	*15:06
Can	27	*16:27
Leo	29	*21:26
Vir	2	*06:12
Lib	4	*17:42
Sco	7	*06:15
Sag	9	*18:42
Cap	12	*06:13
Aqu	14	*15:50
Pis	16	*22:30
Ari	19	*01:46

1964		
Leo	19	*05:39
Vir	21	*11:18
Lib	23	*19:08
Sco	26	*05:00
Sag	28	*16:45
Cap	1	*05:42
Aqu	3	*18:06
Pis	6	*03:42
Ari	8	*09:14
Tau	10	*11:38
Gem	12	*11:01
Can	14	*10:54
Leo	16	*12:32
Vir	18	*17:02

♉ Taurus – Finding Your Moon Sign ☽

1965		
Cap	21	*01:24
Aqu	23	*14:03
Pis	26	*02:01
Ari	28	*11:10
Tau	30	*17:03
Gem	2	*20:26
Can	4	*22:38
Leo	7	*00:49
Vir	9	*03:47
Lib	11	*08:04
Sco	13	*14:10
Sag	15	*22:32
Cap	18	*09:20
Aqu	20	*21:50

1966		
Tau	20	*19:59
Gem	23	*04:26
Can	25	*10:46
Leo	27	*15:08
Vir	29	*17:49
Lib	1	*19:30
Sco	3	*21:23
Sag	6	*00:53
Cap	8	*07:12
Aqu	10	*16:51
Pis	13	*04:54
Ari	15	*17:15
Tau	18	*03:48
Gem	20	*11:38

1967		
Vir	20	*05:42
Lib	22	*06:41
Sco	24	*06:18
Sag	26	*06:26
Cap	28	*08:54
Aqu	30	*14:58
Pis	3	*00:47
Ari	5	*13:09
Tau	8	*02:09
Gem	10	*14:07
Can	13	*00:09
Leo	15	*07:48
Vir	17	*12:50
Lib	19	*15:30

1968		
Aqu	19	*19:57
Pis	22	*02:46
Ari	24	*12:32
Tau	27	*00:22
Gem	29	*13:10
Can	2	*01:49
Leo	4	*12:52
Vir	6	*20:57
Lib	9	*01:19
Sco	11	*02:28
Sag	13	*01:53
Cap	15	*01:31
Aqu	17	*03:22
Pis	19	*08:53

1969		
Gem	19	*10:28
Can	21	*22:17
Leo	24	*10:50
Vir	26	*21:55
Lib	29	*05:43
Sco	1	*09:48
Sag	3	*11:18
Cap	5	*11:57
Aqu	7	*13:28
Pis	9	*17:04
Ari	11	*23:09
Tau	14	*07:28
Gem	16	*17:41
Can	19	*05:30

♉ Taurus – Finding Your Moon Sign ☽

1970		
Sco	21	*14:14
Sag	23	*20:14
Cap	26	*00:25
Aqu	28	*03:42
Pis	30	*06:37
Ari	2	*09:32
Tau	4	*13:05
Gem	6	*18:17
Can	9	*02:17
Leo	11	*13:22
Vir	14	*02:10
Lib	16	*14:01
Sco	18	*22:48

1971		
Pis	20	*20:06
Ari	22	*21:07
Tau	24	*21:06
Gem	26	*21:59
Can	29	*01:44
Leo	1	*09:35
Vir	3	*21:03
Lib	6	*09:58
Sco	8	*22:02
Sag	11	*08:07
Cap	13	*16:08
Aqu	15	*22:18
Pis	18	*02:38
Ari	20	*05:10

1972		
Leo	20	*11:47
Vir	22	*20:24
Lib	25	*07:34
Sco	27	*19:55
Sag	30	*08:30
Cap	2	*20:28
Aqu	5	*06:34
Pis	7	*13:26
Ari	9	*16:34
Tau	11	*16:47
Gem	13	*15:57
Can	15	*16:16
Leo	17	*19:38
Vir	20	*02:56

1973		
Sag	20	*06:01
Cap	22	*18:48
Aqu	25	*07:20
Pis	27	*17:09
Ari	29	*22:51
Tau	2	*01:00
Gem	4	*01:15
Can	6	*01:35
Leo	8	*03:36
Vir	10	*08:13
Lib	12	*15:31
Sco	15	*01:09
Sag	17	*12:41
Cap	20	*01:29

1974		
Ari	20	*00:18
Tau	22	*06:53
Gem	24	*11:10
Can	26	*14:17
Leo	28	*17:03
Vir	30	*20:00
Lib	2	*23:39
Sco	5	*04:43
Sag	7	*12:06
Cap	9	*22:15
Aqu	12	*10:34
Pis	14	*23:02
Ari	17	*09:18
Tau	19	*16:09

♉ Taurus – Finding Your Moon Sign ☽

1975		
Vir	21	*09:41
Lib	23	*10:41
Sco	25	*11:40
Sag	27	*14:20
Cap	29	*20:09
Aqu	2	*05:33
Pis	4	*17:34
Ari	7	*06:02
Tau	9	*17:03
Gem	12	*01:43
Can	14	*08:07
Leo	16	*12:37
Vir	18	*15:45
Lib	20	*18:04

1976		
Aqu	21	*04:47
Pis	23	*14:28
Ari	26	*02:36
Tau	28	*15:37
Gem	1	*04:04
Can	3	*14:52
Leo	5	*23:08
Vir	8	*04:20
Lib	10	*06:39
Sco	12	*07:02
Sag	14	*07:04
Cap	16	*08:32
Aqu	18	*13:03
Pis	20	*21:27

1977		
Gem	21	*02:37
Can	23	*15:24
Leo	26	*02:42
Vir	28	*10:50
Lib	30	*15:11
Sco	2	*16:23
Sag	4	*15:58
Cap	6	*15:54
Aqu	8	*17:59
Pis	10	*23:30
Ari	13	*08:29
Tau	15	*20:04
Gem	18	*08:50
Can	20	*21:35

1978		
Lib	20	*18:52
Sco	22	*23:37
Sag	25	*01:59
Cap	27	*03:27
Aqu	29	*05:27
Pis	1	*09:00
Ari	3	*14:27
Tau	5	*21:52
Gem	8	*07:18
Can	10	*18:41
Leo	13	*07:16
Vir	15	*19:14
Lib	18	*04:23
Sco	20	*09:37

1979		
Aqu	19	*20:01
Pis	21	*22:40
Ari	24	*00:51
Tau	26	*03:27
Gem	28	*07:49
Can	30	*15:12
Leo	3	*01:56
Vir	5	*14:41
Lib	8	*02:46
Sco	10	*12:08
Sag	12	*18:24
Cap	14	*22:25
Aqu	17	*01:25
Pis	19	*04:18

♉ Taurus – Finding Your Moon Sign ☽

1980

Leo	21	*22:52
Vir	24	*10:12
Lib	26	*23:09
Sco	29	*11:34
Sag	1	*22:21
Cap	4	*07:13
Aqu	6	*14:02
Pis	8	*18:33
Ari	10	*20:43
Tau	12	*21:24
Gem	14	*22:08
Can	17	*00:53
Leo	19	*07:14

1981

Sag	21	*22:14
Cap	24	*10:30
Aqu	26	*20:55
Pis	29	*03:55
Ari	1	*06:56
Tau	3	*06:59
Gem	5	*06:00
Can	7	*06:17
Leo	9	*09:41
Vir	11	*16:55
Lib	14	*03:24
Sco	16	*15:37
Sag	19	*04:13

1982

Ari	21	*12:21
Tau	23	*14:58
Gem	25	*15:48
Can	27	*16:43
Leo	29	*19:09
Vir	1	*23:45
Lib	4	*06:32
Sco	6	*15:24
Sag	9	*02:17
Cap	11	*14:49
Aqu	14	*03:43
Pis	16	*14:45
Ari	18	*22:02

1983

Leo	20	*09:26
Vir	22	*12:11
Lib	24	*15:03
Sco	26	*19:04
Sag	29	*01:29
Cap	1	*11:01
Aqu	3	*23:09
Pis	6	*11:42
Ari	8	*22:15
Tau	11	*05:35
Gem	13	*10:02
Can	15	*12:47
Leo	17	*15:00
Vir	19	*17:36

1984

Cap	20	*09:11
Aqu	22	*18:27
Pis	25	*06:26
Ari	27	*19:02
Tau	30	*06:30
Gem	2	*16:01
Can	4	*23:25
Leo	7	*04:42
Vir	9	*08:01
Lib	11	*09:53
Sco	13	*11:22
Sag	15	*13:50
Cap	17	*18:43
Aqu	20	*02:56

♉ Taurus – Finding Your Moon Sign ☽

1985		
Tau	20	*05:12
Gem	22	*18:00
Can	25	*05:25
Leo	27	*14:08
Vir	29	*19:23
Lib	1	*21:21
Sco	3	*21:16
Sag	5	*20:56
Cap	7	*22:12
Aqu	10	*02:38
Pis	12	*10:56
Ari	14	*22:25
Tau	17	*11:23
Gem	20	*00:00

1986		
Vir	20	*00:22
Lib	22	*04:49
Sco	24	*06:15
Sag	26	*06:16
Cap	28	*06:40
Aqu	30	*09:06
Pis	2	*14:31
Ari	4	*23:01
Tau	7	*09:59
Gem	9	*22:25
Can	12	*11:17
Leo	14	*23:14
Vir	17	*08:44
Lib	19	*14:39

1987		
Pis	23	*01:02
Ari	25	*05:40
Tau	27	*12:06
Gem	29	*20:43
Can	2	*07:39
Leo	4	*20:06
Vir	7	*08:06
Lib	9	*17:28
Sco	11	*23:07
Sag	14	*01:40
Cap	16	*02:36
Aqu	18	*03:42
Pis	20	*06:24

1988		
Can	21	*04:05
Leo	23	*14:34
Vir	26	*03:15
Lib	28	*15:36
Sco	1	*01:38
Sag	3	*08:51
Cap	5	*13:53
Aqu	7	*17:36
Pis	9	*20:38
Ari	11	*23:23
Tau	14	*02:22
Gem	16	*06:31
Can	18	*13:06
Leo	20	*22:52

1989		
Sco	21	*01:12
Sag	23	*12:37
Cap	25	*22:14
Aqu	28	*05:32
Pis	30	*10:02
Ari	2	*11:49
Tau	4	*11:54
Gem	6	*12:04
Can	8	*14:20
Leo	10	*20:23
Vir	13	*06:30
Lib	15	*19:07
Sco	18	*07:47
Sag	20	*18:51

♉ Taurus – Finding Your Moon Sign ☽

1990		
Pis	20	*17:56
Ari	22	*20:57
Tau	24	*21:02
Gem	26	*20:12
Can	28	*20:39
Leo	1	*00:09
Vir	3	*07:18
Lib	5	*17:28
Sco	8	*05:22
Sag	10	*17:56
Cap	13	*06:20
Aqu	15	*17:29
Pis	18	*01:52
Ari	20	*06:31

1991		
Leo	21	*11:04
Vir	23	*15:29
Lib	25	*21:36
Sco	28	*05:33
Sag	30	*15:42
Cap	3	*03:54
Aqu	5	*16:50
Pis	8	*04:03
Ari	10	*11:33
Tau	12	*15:06
Gem	14	*16:01
Can	16	*16:13
Leo	18	*17:30
Vir	20	*21:00

1992		
Sag	19	*14:41
Cap	21	*23:41
Aqu	24	*11:38
Pis	27	*00:19
Ari	29	*11:12
Tau	1	*19:08
Gem	4	*00:27
Can	6	*04:09
Leo	8	*07:07
Vir	10	*09:56
Lib	12	*13:05
Sco	14	*17:15
Sag	16	*23:22
Cap	19	*08:13

1993		
Ari	19	*08:14
Tau	21	*20:07
Gem	24	*06:26
Can	26	*14:44
Leo	28	*20:38
Vir	30	*23:58
Lib	3	*01:19
Sco	5	*01:57
Sag	7	*03:35
Cap	9	*07:51
Aqu	11	*15:44
Pis	14	*02:50
Ari	16	*15:23
Tau	19	*03:15

1994		
Vir	21	*09:56
Lib	23	*11:39
Sco	25	*11:18
Sag	27	*10:48
Cap	29	*12:06
Aqu	1	*16:34
Pis	4	*00:47
Ari	6	*12:01
Tau	9	*00:50
Gem	11	*13:43
Can	14	*01:26
Leo	16	*10:57
Vir	18	*17:30
Lib	20	*20:53

111

♉ Taurus – Finding Your Moon Sign ☽

1995		
Cap	19	*21:54
Aqu	22	*00:38
Pis	24	*05:50
Ari	26	*13:41
Tau	28	*23:53
Gem	1	*11:53
Can	4	*00:44
Leo	6	*12:54
Vir	8	*22:32
Lib	11	*04:29
Sco	13	*06:52
Sag	15	*06:58
Cap	17	*06:35
Aqu	19	*07:39

1996		
Gem	20	*09:54
Can	22	*20:25
Leo	25	*08:44
Vir	27	*20:48
Lib	30	*06:26
Sco	2	*12:41
Sag	4	*16:04
Cap	6	*17:53
Aqu	8	*19:38
Pis	10	*22:29
Ari	13	*03:00
Tau	15	*09:25
Gem	17	*17:47
Can	20	*04:16

1997		
Lib	20	*04:36
Sco	22	*15:18
Sag	24	*23:31
Cap	27	*05:32
Aqu	29	*09:49
Pis	1	*12:49
Ari	3	*14:58
Tau	5	*17:04
Gem	7	*20:21
Can	10	*02:13
Leo	12	*11:33
Vir	14	*23:43
Lib	17	*12:26
Sco	19	*23:10

1998		
Aqu	19	*20:40
Pis	22	*01:04
Ari	24	*02:29
Tau	26	*02:08
Gem	28	*01:56
Can	30	*03:57
Leo	2	*09:50
Vir	4	*19:47
Lib	7	*08:18
Sco	9	*21:09
Sag	12	*08:47
Cap	14	*18:38
Aqu	17	*02:29
Pis	19	*08:02

1999		
Can	20	*11:28
Leo	22	*15:06
Vir	24	*22:04
Lib	27	*07:46
Sco	29	*19:12
Sag	2	*07:36
Cap	4	*20:11
Aqu	7	*07:39
Pis	9	*16:15
Ari	11	*20:51
Tau	13	*21:55
Gem	15	*21:07
Can	17	*20:40
Leo	19	*22:38

2000		
Sag	21	*04:57
Cap	23	*16:47
Aqu	26	*05:41
Pis	28	*17:05
Ari	1	*00:53
Tau	3	*04:53
Gem	5	*06:23
Can	7	*07:13
Leo	9	*09:01
Vir	11	*12:41
Lib	13	*18:27
Sco	16	*02:16
Sag	18	*12:09

♉ Taurus Mercury Signs ☿

	ARIES	TAURUS	GEMINI
1930		Apr 19–May 1	May 1–May 17
		May 17–May 21	
1931		Apr 19–May 21	
1932	Apr 19–May 15	May 15–May 21	
1933	Apr 19–May 10	May 10–May 21	
1934	Apr 19–May 2	May 2–May 16	May 16–May 21
1935	Apr 19–Apr 24	Apr 24–May 8	May 8–May 21
1936		Apr 19–May 1	May 1–May 21
1937		Apr 19–May 21	
1938	Apr 23 – May 16	Apr 19–Apr 23	
		May 16–May 21	
1939	Apr 19–May 14	May 14–May 21	
1940	Apr 19–May 6	May 6–May 21	
1941	Apr 19–Apr 28	Apr 28–May 13	May 13 –21
1942		Apr 20–May 5	May 5–May 21
1943		Apr 20–Apr 30	Apr 30–May 21
1944	Apr 20 –May 21		
1945	Apr 20–May 16	May 16–May 21	
1946	Apr 20–May 11	May 11–May 21	
1947	Apr 20– May 4	May 4–May 18	May 18–May 21
1948	Apr 20–Apr 25	Apr 25–May 9	May 9–May 21
1949	Apr 20–May 2		May 2–May 21
1950		Apr 20–May 21	
1951	May 1–May 15	Apr 20–May 1	
		May 15–May 21	
1952	Apr 20–May 14	May 14–May 21	
1953	Apr 19–May 8	May 8–May 21	
1954	Apr 19–Apr 30	Apr 30–May 14	May 14–May 21
1955	Apr 20–Apr 22	Apr 22–May 6	May 6–May 21

	ARIES	TAURUS	GEMINI
1956		Apr 20–Apr 29	Apr 29–May 21
1957		Apr 20–May 21	
1958	Apr 19–May 17	May 17–May 21	
1959	Apr 20–May 12 1	May 12–May 21	
1960	Apr 19–May 4	May 4–May 19	May 19–May 21
1961	Apr 20–Apr 26	Apr 26–May 10	May 10–May 21
1962		Apr 20 –May 3	May 3–May 21
1963		Apr 20–May 3 & May 10–May 21	May 3–May 10
1964		Apr 20–May 21	
1965	Apr 20–May 15	May 15–May 21	
1966	Apr 20–May 9	May 9–May 21	
1967	Apr 20–May 1	May 1–May 16	May 16–May 21
1968	Apr 20–Apr 22	Apr 22–May 6	May 6–May 21
1969		Apr 20–Apr 30	Apr 30–May 21
1970		Apr 20–May 21	
1971	Apr 19–May 17	May 17–May 21	
1972	Apr 20–May 12	May 12–May 21	
1973	Apr 20–May 6	May 6–May 21	
1974	Apr 20–Apr 28	Apr 28–May 12	May 12–May 21
1975		Apr 19–May 4	May 4–May 21
1976		Apr 20–Apr 29 May 19–May 21	Apr 29–May 19
1977		Apr 20–May 21	
1978	Apr 20–May 16	May 16–May 21	
1979	Apr 20–May 10	May 10–May 21	
1980	Apr 20–May 2	May 2–May 16	May 16–May 21
1981	Apr 20–Apr 24	Apr 24–May 8	May 8–May 21
1982		Apr 20–May 1	May 1–May 21
1983		Apr 20–May 21	

	ARIES	TAURUS	GEMINI
1984	Apr 25–May 15	Apr 20–Apr 25	
		May 15–May 21	
1985	Apr 20–May 14	May 14–May 21	
1986	Apr 20–May 7	May 7–May 21	
1987	Apr 20–Apr 29	Apr 29–May 13	May 13–May 21
1988		Apr 20–May 4	May 4–May 21
1989		Apr 19–Apr 29	Apr 29–May 21
1990		Apr 19–May 21	
1991	Apr 19–May 16	May 16–May 21	
1992	Apr 19–May 11	May 11- May 21	
1993	Apr 19–May 3	May 3–May 18	May 18–May 21
1994	Apr 19–Apr 25	Apr 25–May 9	May 9–May 21
1995		Apr 19–May 2	May 2–May 21
1996		Apr 19–May 21	
1997	May 5–May 12	Apr 19–May 5	
		May 12–May 21	
1998	Apr 19–May 15	May 15–May 21	
1999	Apr 19–May 8	May 8–May 21	
2000	Apr 19–Apr 30	Apr 30–May 14	May 14- May 21

♉ Taurus Venus Signs ♀

YEAR	PISCES	ARIES	TAURUS	GEMINI	CANCER
1930			20 Apr–30Apr	30 Apr–21 May	
1931	20 Apr–26 Apr	26 Apr –21 May			
1932				20 Apr–6 May	6 May–21 May
1933	20 Apr–6 May	20 Apr	20 Apr–15 May	15 May–21 May	
1934		6 May–21 May		20 Apr–11 May	11 May–21 May
1935			5 May–21 May		
1936		20 Apr–5 May			
1937		20 Apr–21 May			
1938	20 Apr–25 Apr		20 Apr–29 Apr	29 Apr–21 May	
1939		25 Apr–20 May	20 May –21 May		6 May–21 May
1940				20 Apr–6 May	
1941	20 Apr–6 May	20 Apr–14 May	14 May–21 May		
1942		6 May–21 May		20 Apr–11 May	11 May–21 May
1943			20 Apr–21 May	20 Apr–11 May	
1944					
1945		20 Apr–21 May			
1946		25 Apr–21 May	20 Apr–29 Apr	29 Apr–21 May	
1947	20 Apr–25 Apr			20 Apr–7 May	7 May–21 May
1948				20 Apr–7 May	
1949			20 Apr–14 May	14 May–21 May	
1950	20 Apr–5 May	5 May–21 May			
1951				20 Apr–11 May	11 Amy–21 May

YEAR	PISCES	ARIES	TAURUS	GEMINI	CANCER
1952		20 Apr–4 May	4 May–21 May		
1953		20 Apr–21 May			
1954				28 Apr–21 May	
1955	21 Apr–24 Apr	24 Apr–19 May	20 Apr–28 Apr		8 May–21 May
1956			19 May–21 May	20 Apr–8 May	
1957	20 Apr–5 May	5 May–21May	20 Apr–13 May	13 May–21 May	
1958				20 Apr–10 May	10 May–21 May
1959					
1960		20 Apr–3 May	3 May–21 May		
1961		20 Apr–21 May			
1962			20 Apr–28 Apr	28 Apr–21 May	
1963	20 Apr–24 Apr	24 Apr–19 May	19 May–21 May		9 May–21 May
1964				20 Apr–9 May	
1965			20 Apr–12 May	12 May–21 May	
1966	20 Apr–12 May	12 May–21 May			10 May–21 May
1967				20 Apr–10 May	
1968		20 Apr–3 May	3 May–21 May		
1969		20 Apr–21 May			
1970			20 Apr–27 Apr	27 Apr–21 May	
1971	20 Apr–23 Apr	23 Apr–18 May	18 May–21 May		10 May–21 May
1972				20 Apr–10 May	
1973			20 Apr–12 May	12 May–21 May	
1974	20 Apr–4 May	4 May–21 May			9 May–21 May
1975					
1976	20 Apr–2 May	20 Apr–2 May	2 May–21 May	20 Apr–9 May	

YEAR	PISCES	ARIES	TAURUS	GEMINI	CANCER
1977		20 Apr–21 May	20 Apr–27 Apr	27 Apr–21 May	
1978					
1979	20 Apr–23 Apr	23 Apr–21 May			12 May–21 May
1980			20 Apr–11 May	20 Apr–12 May	
1981				11 May–21 May	
1982	20 Apr–4 May	4 May–21 May		20 Apr–9 May	9 May–21 May
1983			2 May–21 May		
1984		20 Apr–2 May			
1985		20 Apr–21 May			
1986			20 Apr–26 Apr	26 Apr–21 May	
1987	20 Apr–22 Apr	22 Apr–17 May	17 May–21 May		17 May–21 May
1988				20 Apr–17 May	
1989			20 Apr–11 May	11 May–21 May	
1990	20 Apr–4 May	4 May–21 May		20 Apr–9 May	9 May–21 May
1991			1 May–21 May		
1992		20 Apr–1 May			
1993		20 Apr–21 May			
1994	20 Apr–22 Apr	22 Apr–16 May	20 Apr–26 Apr	26 Apr–21 May	
1995			16 May–21 May		
1996			20 Apr–10 May	20 Apr–21 May	
1997				10 May–21 May	
1998	20 Apr–8 May	8 May–21 May		20 Apr–8 May	8 May–21 May
1999			1 May–21 May		
2000		20 Apr–1 May			

The Taurus Workbook

There are no right or wrong answers in this chapter. Its aim is to help you assess how you are doing with your life – in YOUR estimation – and to make the material of this book more personal and, I hope, more helpful for you.

1. The Taurus in You

Which of the following Taurus characteristics do you recognise in yourself?

calm	sensual	steadfast	contented
appreciative	practical	peaceful	patient
reliable	down-to-earth	strong-willed	prudent
nature-loving	persevering	productive	music-loving

2. In which situations do you find yourself acting like this?

_____

_____

3. When you are feeling vulnerable, you may show some of the less constructive Taurus traits. Do you recognise yourself in any of the following?

controlling	possessive	boring
intolerant	stubborn	blunt
dictatorial	materialistic	procrastinating

What kind of situations trigger off this behaviour and what do you think might help you, in these situations, to respond more positively?

_____

_____

4. You and Your Roles
a) Where, if anywhere, in your life do you play the role of Steward?

_____

_____

b) What resources do you take care of?

_____

_____

5. Do you play any of the following roles – in the literal or broad sense – in any part of your life? If not, would you like to? What might be your first step towards doing so?

Artist   Builder   Controller
Gardener   Peacemaker   Gourmet

_____

_____

6. Sun Aspects
If any of the following planets aspects your Sun, add each of the keywords for that planet to complete the following sentences. Which phrases ring true for you?

I am _____

My father is _____

My job requires that I am _____

Saturn Words (Use only if your Sun is aspected by Saturn)

ambitious	controlling	judgmental	mature
serious	strict	traditional	bureaucratic
cautious	committed	hard-working	disciplined
depressive	responsible	status-seeking	limiting

Uranus Words (Use only if your Sun is aspected by Uranus)

freedom-loving	progressive	rebellious	shocking
scientific	cutting-edge	detached	contrary
friendly	disruptive	eccentric	humanitarian
innovative	nonconformist	unconventional	exciting

Neptune Words (Use only if your Sun is aspected by Neptune)

sensitive	idealistic	artistic	impressionable
disappointing	impractical	escapist	self-sacrificing
spiritual	unrealistic	dreamy	glamorous
dependent	deceptive	rescuing	blissful

Pluto Words (Use only if your Sun is aspected by Pluto)

powerful	single-minded	intense	extreme
secretive	rotten	passionate	mysterious
investigative	uncompromising	ruthless	wealthy
abusive	regenerative	associated with sex, birth or death	

a) If one or more negative words describe you or your job, how might you turn that quality into something more positive or satisfying?

_____

_____

7. The Moon and You

Below are brief lists of what the Moon needs, in the various elements, to feel secure and satisfied. First find your Moon element, then estimate how much of each of the following you are expressing and receiving in your life, especially at home and in your relationships, on a scale of 0 to 5 where 0 = none and 5 = plenty.

FIRE MOONS — Aries, Leo, Sagittarius

attention	action	drama
recognition	self-expression	spontaneity
enthusiasm	adventure	leadership

EARTH MOONS — Taurus, Virgo, Capricorn

stability	orderly routine	sensual pleasures
material security	a sense of rootedness	control over your home life
regular body care	practical achievements	pleasurable practical tasks

AIR MOONS — Gemini, Libra, Aquarius

mental rapport	stimulating ideas	emotional space
friendship	social justice	interesting conversations
fairness	socialising	freedom to circulate

WATER MOONS — Cancer, Scorpio, Pisces

intimacy	a sense of belonging	emotional rapport
emotional safety	respect for your feelings	time and space to retreat
acceptance	cherishing and being cherished	warmth and comfort

a) Do you feel your Moon is being 'fed' enough?

yes_____ no_____

b) How might you satisfy your Moon needs even better?

_____

_____

8. You and Your Mercury

As a Taurean, your Mercury can only be in Aries, Taurus or Gemini. Below are some of the ways and situations in which Mercury in each of the elements might learn and communicate effectively. First find your Mercury sign, then circle the words you think apply to you.

Mercury in Fire (Aries)

action	imagination	identifying with the subject matter
excitement	drama	playing with possibilities

Mercury in Earth (Taurus)

time-tested methods	useful facts	well-structured information
'how to' instructions	demonstrations	hands-on experience

Mercury in Air (Gemini)

facts arranged in categories	logic	demonstrable connections
rational arguments	theories	debate and sharing of ideas

Mercury in Water (As a Taurean, you can never have Mercury in a water sign; the words are included here for completeness)

pictures and images	charged atmospheres	feeling-linked information
intuitive understanding	emotional rapport	being shown personally

a) This game with Mercury can be done with a friend or on

your own. Skim through a magazine until you find a picture that interests you. Then describe the picture – to your friend, or in writing or on tape. Notice what you emphasise and the kind of words you use. Now try to describe it using the language and emphasis of each of the other Mercury modes. How easy did you find that? Identifying the preferred Mercury style of others and using that style yourself can lead to improved communication all round.

9. Your Venus Values
Below are lists of qualities and situations that your Venus sign might enjoy. Assess on a scale of 0 to 5 how much your Venus desires and pleasures are met and expressed in your life. 0 = not at all, 5 = fully.

Venus in Aries
You will activate your Venus by taking part in anything that makes you feel potent, for example:

taking the initiative   competition   risk-taking
action dramas   taking the lead   tough challenges

Venus in Taurus
You will activate your Venus through whatever pleases the senses and enhances your sense of stability, for example:

financial security   beauty   gardening and nature
sensual pleasures   good food   body pampering

Venus in Gemini

You will activate your Venus through anything that stimulates your mind and uses a talent for making connections, for example:

playing go-between	flirting	talking and writing
passing on new ideas	witty use of words	trend-spotting

Venus in Cancer

You will activate your Venus through anything that makes you feel wise, intuitive, nurturing and nurtured, and at the centre of a 'family', for example:

a beautiful home	tenderness	sharing meals with loved ones
sharing feelings safely	home comforts	your family or country history

Venus in Pisces

You will activate your Venus through anything that allows you to experience fusion with something greater than yourself, for example:

relieving suffering	daydreaming	creating a glamorous image
spiritual devotion	voluntary service	losing yourself in art, music or love

a) How, and where, might you have more fun and pleasure by bringing more of what your Venus sign loves into your life?

_____

_____

b) Make a note here of the kind of gifts your Venus sign would love to receive. Then go on and spoil yourself . . .

_____

Resources

Finding an Astrologer

I'm often asked what is the best way to find a reputable astrologer. Personal recommendation by someone whose judgement you trust is by far the best way. Ideally, the astrologer should also be endorsed by a reputable organisation whose members adhere to a strict code of ethics, which guarantees confidentiality and professional conduct.

Contact Addresses

Association of Professional Astrologers
www.professionalastrologers.org

APA members adhere to a strict code of professional ethics.

Astrological Association of Great Britain
www.astrologicalassociation.co.uk

The main body for astrology in the UK that also has information on astrological events and organisations throughout the world.

Faculty of Astrological Studies
www.astrology.org.uk

The teaching body internationally recognised for excellence in astrological education at all levels.

Your Taurean Friends

You can keep a record of Taureans you know here, with the page numbers of where to find their descriptions handy for future reference.

Name _____ Date of Birth _____

Aspects*	None	Saturn	Uranus	Neptune	Pluto
Moon Sign _____				p _____	
Mercury Sign _____				p _____	
Venus Sign _____				p _____	

Name _____ Date of Birth _____

Aspects*	None	Saturn	Uranus	Neptune	Pluto
Moon Sign _____				p _____	
Mercury Sign _____				p _____	
Venus Sign _____				p _____	

Name _____ Date of Birth _____

Aspects*	None	Saturn	Uranus	Neptune	Pluto
Moon Sign _____				p _____	
Mercury Sign _____				p _____	
Venus Sign _____				p _____	

Name _____ Date of Birth _____

Aspects*	None	Saturn	Uranus	Neptune	Pluto
Moon Sign _____				p _____	
Mercury Sign _____				p _____	
Venus Sign _____				p _____	

* Circle where applicable

Sign Summaries

SIGN	GLYPH	APPROX DATES	SYMBOL	ROLE	ELEMENT	QUALITY	PLANET	GLYPH	KEYWORD
1. Aries	♈	21/3 – 19/4	Ram	Hero	Fire	Cardinal	Mars	♂	Assertiveness
2. Taurus	♉	20/4 – 20/5	Bull	Steward	Earth	Fixed	Venus	♀	Stability
3. Gemini	♊	21/5 – 21/6	Twins	Go-Between	Air	Mutable	Mercury	☿	Communication
4. Cancer	♋	22/6 – 22/7	Crab	Caretaker	Water	Cardinal	Moon	☽	Nurture
5. Leo	♌	23/7 – 22/8	Lion	Performer	Fire	Fixed	Sun	☉	Glory
6. Virgo	♍	23/8 – 22/9	Maiden	Craftworker	Earth	Mutable	Mercury	☿	Skill
7. Libra	♎	23/9 – 22/10	Scales	Architect	Air	Cardinal	Venus	♀	Balance
8. Scorpio	♏	23/10 – 23/11	Scorpion	Survivor	Water	Fixed	Pluto	♇	Transformation
9. Sagittarius	♐	22/11 – 21/12	Archer	Adventurer	Fire	Mutable	Jupiter	♃	Wisdom
10. Capricorn	♑	22/12 – 19/1	Goat	Manager	Earth	Cardinal	Saturn	♄	Responsibility
11. Aquarius	♒	20/1 – 19/2	Waterbearer	Scientist	Air	Fixed	Uranus	♅	Progress
12. Pisces	♓	20/2 – 20/3	Fishes	Dreamer	Water	Mutable	Neptune	♆	Universality